SHOOTING THE WORKS

BOOKS BY W. S. DI PIERO

Poetry

The First Hour
The Only Dangerous Thing
Early Light
The Dog Star
The Restorers
Shadows Burning

Essays

Memory and Enthusiasm
Out of Eden

Translations

Pensieri, by Giacomo Leopardi
This Strange Joy: Selected Poems of Sandro Penna
The Ellipse: Selected Poems of Leonardo Sinisgalli
Ion, by Euripides

· *W. S. Di Piero* ·

SHOOTING
on poetry and pictures
THE WORKS

TRIQUARTERLY BOOKS
NORTHWESTERN UNIVERSITY PRESS

Evanston, Illinois

TriQuarterly Books

Northwestern University Press

Evanston, Illinois 60208-4210

Library of Congress Cataloging-in-Publication Data

Di Piero, W. S.

    Shooting the works : on poetry and pictures / W.S. Di Piero.

        p. cm.

    Collection of essays originally published 1989–1994.

    Includes index.

    ISBN 0-8101-5051-4 (alk. paper). — ISBN 0-8101-5052-2 (pbk. :

alk. paper)

     I. Title.

PS3554.I65S53   1996

814'.54—dc20   95-51559

                                            CIP

CONTENTS

· **III** ·

PREFACE

I wrote these essays between 1989 and 1994, though I have not arranged them chronologically. (The year of publication for most of them can be found in the Acknowledgments.) Likewise, the paragraphs included in Part 3, "Out of Notebooks," made up of material from my notebooks that I've cleaned up a bit to make presentable here, do not appear in chronological sequence, though they all come from the same 1989–94 period. I thank the two editors who in recent years have been most important to me. Reginald Gibbons of TriQuarterly Books took over my poetry and prose when I had no publisher. His faith saved me. Wendy Lesser of *Threepenny Review* has for ten years given my work the great gift of her friendship. She does not know how much her good will and enthusiasm—kind words zooming out of nowhere!—have sustained me.

ACKNOWLEDGMENTS

Much of the material in this book first appeared in the
following magazines and books:

The New England Review (1993)
"Pocketbook and Sauerkraut"

Southwest Review (1993)
"Poetry in Common"

The Columbia History of American Poetry
(Columbia University Press, 1993)
"Public Music"

The New England Review (1996)
"The Tactics and Strategy of Thomas McGrath"

Seneca Review (1990)
"A Note on Hayden Carruth and Personality"

Chicago Review (1990)
"On Edwin Muir"

TriQuarterly, a publication of Northwestern University (1993)
"Shooting the Works"

Threepenny Review (1994)
"Gots Is What You Got"

Hudson Review (1991)
"Restorations"

Epoch (1992)
"On Paul Resika"

National Gallery of Art Publications (1994)
"HOLD STILL KEEP GOING"

The Gettysburg Review (1992)
"Seeker and Finder: Minor White and Lee Freidlander"

Epoch (1994)
"Ten Takes"

Three sections from "Out of Notebooks" first appeared in *Threepenny Review* (1993) and *Manoa* (1995).

I'm grateful to Christian Wiman for his close reading of this book and
for the many helpful changes he suggested.

· I ·

Pocketbook and Sauerkraut

1

I did not know I was a member of the working class until I no longer was. In the dense Italian neighborhood in South Philadelphia where I grew up, there were no class distinctions because we were all one socioeconomic group. The men with skilled trades made out a little better than those like my father whose lack of training qualified them at best for low level general maintenance jobs. The skilled workers might own a bigger TV set or have a taller fir tree in their parlors at Christmas, and the only boy who owned a football was the son of a workingman employed in the mysterious and relatively new field called electronics, clean work, the only kind of work we saw advertised on TV in General Electric commercials. Progress is our most important product, it said. The sense of that slogan meant nothing to me as a child, but the tune the words made, the canter of the pentameter, held in my mind as a beautiful pattern.

One street down, across 21st Street, on the next block of Watkins, lived the only people spoken of as a different, inferior class. The black working people and their children rarely crossed over into our neighborhood. Though physically closer to us than any other group, in language they were demonized and made the most remote and adversarial. Ethnic and racial tags made up our richest vocabulary. As tribes often have many names for the most critical presence in their communal life—twenty words for snow or river or salmon—we all had words to fix and set apart *the others*. The black boys who sometimes crossed over in gangs and jumped us would chant the names: Guinea, Boone, Greaser, Whitey, Wop. And we had names for them: Spook, Rubberhead, Jigaboo, Mul'. Where did "Boone" come from? What dialect turned *melanzana*, "eggplant," into *mulagnam'*, shortened to *mul'* and pronounced "mool"? I loved the loose, slippery textures of those words as much as I clenched inside with fear and disgust to hear them used. But I also sensed that to reject the language of the tribe was to risk rejecting its identity and reality in the world. Reject the words and you were in some way acting to kill off your own people, casting yourself into an exile of prideful superiority. There grew in me a child's conviction that language was a locked box in which were stored the most irrational, alienating, and violent voices. The most puzzling thing of all was the discrepancy between the censoring otherness words attached to our working-class black neighbors and the reality my eye took in. Our block was clean but colorless and drab, without ornament: redbrick rowhouses, granite front steps, and a single large sycamore. One block down, however, they had planters in front of their houses, more trees, too, and windowboxes that splashed the distant air with wonderful colors. On our block, I hardly ever saw fresh flowers indoors or out. For signs of joy, for Nature, I looked across the 21st Street divide to that *other* place.

Among my people an awareness of ethnic separateness was more important than socioeconomic or political identity. Non-Italians were *americani*, except blacks and Jews. They weren't Americans, either. From the man who worked at G.E. we would hear about black co-workers, whom he spoke of with respect and good will; he was also the only man in the neighborhood to go out on strike. Most of the other men feared a strike because they had too much at risk and tended to be suspicious anyway of anyone outside the family-neighborhood orbit. The G.E. father, however, drew mysterious power from the group, from the mass of workers acting as one entity, one will. The refusal to work, walking off the job, was so out of keeping with the mentality of my neighborhood that to my young mind it seemed at once heroic and insane.

We know ourselves in part by the misrepresentations others make of us. Many years after I'd left Philadelphia, someone I knew pretty well but to whom I'd said little about my early years assumed I grew up in an Italian culture rich with peasant traditions, Verdi on the phonograph, flowers everywhere, Old Master reproductions on the wall, tomatoes ripening in the back yard. In my house there were no flowers, no opera (no phonograph, for that matter), and no images except for devotional bric-a-brac and seething black and white images on TV. There is no peasantry in my background, only village laborers and tradesmen (and, a few generations back, a priest who left his property holdings to the prostitute who bore his child; a professional gambler; a racketeer; and a bigamist who became a boom-to-bust coffee plantation tycoon some-where in South America). Another friend assumed I came from an anar-co-syndicalist background, as if all immigrant laborers were political kin to Sacco and Vanzetti. There was, in fact, never a mention of working classes in my house or neighborhood. There was mostly talk about us Italians and all the *americani*. Until I went to college, where I was taught that there has been no determinant class system in America comparable to those in European nations like Italy, with their historical distinctions among peasant, landowner, subproletariat, proletariat, petit bourgeois, and aristocrat, I had hardly ever met anyone who spoke differently from me, and though I did not know it then, I understood in time that one purpose of American education was to detach me, or enable me to detach myself, from what I was finally learning to call "the working class" into which I was born.

My class awareness, such as it was, came packed in words and speech. I still repeat to myself the rhyme we learned as kids:

> I made you look, you dirty crook,
> I stole your mother's pocketbook.
> I turned it in, I turned it out,
> I turned it into sauerkraut.

Pocketbook and Sauerkraut

The lines live in the same zone and continuity of my consciousness as passages from Dante, the Sermon on the Mount, "To Autumn," "My Last Duchess," "Asphodel, That Greeny Flower," Edgar's speeches in *King Lear*, and Antony's "Sometime we see a cloud that's dragonish." Its words constitute a *mysterium sanctum* where meaning lies in wait for initiates, and where language bleeds together conversation, doggerel, and formal elegance into one way of speech. But you can study, make sacrifice, burn incense, and still not be enlightened, for meaning is also sometimes a surprising gift, a sentence whose rhythms spring like a trap and catch you. At that sanctuary Nimrod is the spectral custodian, always there to break sense into incoherence. But it was, is, my true place. Outside, vendors sold hoagies and pizzasteaks and lemonade. L-e-m-o-n-a-d-e had all the sweetness of sound I expected of the thing. Except that it wasn't really lemonade. Only in my teens did I learn that what we called lemonade was really lemon water ice. Lemonade was, for Americans, a drink! I was set straight by a high school pal, a lawyer's son. I made you look, you dirty crook. My real learning was about the executive power of language to reveal, enchant, disguise, and transgress. Who knows what "education" was being buzzed around my head by the sisters in grade school and the priests in high school? Turning someone's mother's pocketbook into sauerkraut was a power as outlandish and severe in its illusion as Harpo's power at the stringboard. Fantastical and sleight-of-hand, words in patterns had a lightness and buoyant canniness that my culture of labor either had no time for or disdained outright. What my culture did give me was a sense—a tactile, mineral sense—of language as the embodiment of contingency. And I think I also absorbed from my culture other qualities that have served me as a poet, a tenacity and a stupefied willfulness to make words answerable to the densities of consciousness.

But language, of course, was not so nicely patterned or cut to satisfying forms. That's not how I experienced it. It was swampy, crazily shadowed, and pied with unintelligible matter. Its flashes and zigzags and curls pulled me in. One of my uncles, answering the door when I knocked (I was twelve), said: "So what can I sue you for?" Why would he want to sue me? How had he become my enemy? Was he joking? Why joke about suing me and taking away everything I owned? My own uncle! *Sue you for*: force you, sure, or use your four—O Sue, for you! I have never shed that instinct for and anxiety about the incipient babble in sentences. It has made me an unstable and easily confused reader of poetry and a writer of poems whose lines feel as if they are breaking down as soon as they come into a pattern of sense. The anxiety leaked very naturally into my speech as well, so that even now if I'm not attentive it will turn into a slur or mumble, and I am terrified to speak *ex tempore*. The boys in my high school came from different neighborhoods, from Two Street, Grays Ferry, and Ninth and Carpenter, but nearly all came from backgrounds like my own. In college—St. Joseph's, a Jesuit school—I met boys from other backgrounds and places. Some had accents, from the South or Massachusetts or New York, but their speech didn't have the edginess and abrasive candor that sounded so clearly in the tones of Philadelphia working-class boys like myself. I was at ease, and could play the fiction of not speaking with an accent, only when I acted in plays. Otherwise, my bad nerves, uncertainty, and Nimrod anxiety made me too intense. I read with gusto Yeats's remarks in his *Autobiographies* about mastering the rhetorical arts and overcoming shyness. But my culture was massively different from his, and I had no ambitions as a public person; I only wanted to break words and my own speech clear of their roughly shaped origins in my culture.

It did no good anyway. I was reading my Yeats while working long summer hours loading crates with windshields, wheels, doors, and hoods at a Ford Motor Company shipping depot, or else working swing shift at the circuit-breaker factory where by day my mother (widowed several years before) worked on an assembly line. I read Yeats's approval of Axel's remark: "Live? Our servants will do that for us." A society or class that uses servants was, to my nineteen-year-old mind, candyland.

7

To be at ease to do "the real work" of reading and writing! It was fool-ishness, but I've never quite given up that illusion, though I haven't given in to it, either. Sauerkraut and lemonade. Sour lemons aid the Krauts. For you, Sue, I sure can do. Then one night I met a Yeatsian lady, a Main Line sort of Yeatsian lady. After college I worked a succes-sion of menial jobs for a few years. One summer I worked the parking lot at a bandshell in Fairmount Park. One evening, a middle-aged cou-ple in a luxury car ignored my directions and parked in what I soon learned was their favorite (and therefore privileged) spot under a tree. "You remember where we like to park," he said, "and we'll remember you." Confused because tips and unearned privileges had small meaning to me from my previous work experience, I tried to cover my nerves with what I thought were amiable remarks about that evening's Debussy program. The lady, elegantly silent till then, turned to her husband: "What is this person saying? Can *you* understand him?" I quit the job that night. I was twenty-two and about to leave Philadelphia for good. I knew that Yeats was thinking metaphorically, as was Villiers, but only in part. With their aristocratic ambitions, their cult of symbolist disem-bodiment, and their enthrallment to residual forms of nobility wherever they might be found, both poets were writing fact. I could not shake off so suddenly what I was reading and absorbing with such hunger—Yeats seemed a poet who could conquer any tone, speak intensely and formal-ly as one person to another, bring over philosophy into the feeling life of poetry, and his Irishness made him seem archaically foreign—but I did know very soon that I did not want servants doing my living for me, in metaphor or in fact, and that I did not want servants of any kind.

2

In the early 1970s, a few years after my encounter with the Yeatsian concert-goer, I went to live in Italy, where my education in class dis-tinctions continued. It was a tense time. The *contestazione* of 1968 and the years following seemed to have politicized nearly every relation in society, from office to schoolroom to kitchen. The Christian Democratic Party remained the majority party in the coalition government, but for some years the Communist Party under Enrico Berlinguer's leadership had been pursuing its *compromesso storico*, the historic compromise which would lead to the Communist Party's sharing in the coalition. Berlinguer's "communism with a human face" was building its power base not only among the working class but also among the managerial and professional classes. Bologna, where I lived for two years, was a specimen in the experiment. The scene of student and political violence in the 1960s, it was under Communist leadership in the 1970s and becoming the best administered, most congenial and stable local government on the peninsula.

Several of my friends and clients (I survived mainly on private lessons and commercial translation work) were businessmen, professors, and doctors, who voted Communist or Socialist. I lived in a crumbling sixteenth-century building that housed working-class families and tradespeople. The aged lady who lived on the top floor shared a minuscule apartment—there was no central heating in our building—with her nephew; together they operated a produce stand at the local outdoor market. My middle-class friends discussed politics with great seriousness. They fervently supported the struggle of the working class, and they all had servants to clean their houses and prepare their meals. When I said that it seemed a contradiction for Socialists and Communists to keep servants, they readily agreed, for they suffered the contradiction of class privilege versus class affiliation. It confused me to realize that they exercised political passion out of ideological conviction and sympathy, not out of material necessity or inherited grievance. They had grown up among the petite bourgeoisie. In the evening, I would come home from political conversations in spacious, well-furnished apartments and have to help the vegetablemonger carry bags up four flights of stairs to her two-room garret.

Pocketbook and Sauerkraut

In my own way, I was myself a sort of specimen, a true child of the working class, glazed with an American ingenuousness that Italians spotted at once, who also practiced the kind of speculative curiosity and taste for abstraction that they recognized as intellectualism. At the same time, I was trying to make my way as a poet, translator, and literary journalist, which placed me closer to the professional and culture-elite classes than to the working class. I did not fit the picture Italians had of the American social system, where class lines were so liquid and so frequently dissolved under the pressure of "opportunity" that the children of cement-finishers and pipefitters could become lawyers, surgeons, even accountants. (My college's strongest and best endowed program was Food Marketing.) My literary ambitions, however, brought respect from my successful friends and from my upstairs neighbor. I had read Pound's remark that in Europe there was no shame attached to a writer who is poor. My situation caused me both to see and, in a small way, to experience the tense contradictions and guilt that existed within and among the social classes in Italy. My own youthful experience seemed wondrously simple by contrast. During the years I spent in Bologna, a few of the families I was friendly with realized they could no longer live the contradiction, so they released their servants.

One night a few of us went to the premiere of Pasolini's film *The Canterbury Tales*. "We better see it right away," they said. "It's sure to be confiscated as soon as it opens." When we left the theater, the *carabinieri* were waiting in their cars and closed the movie that night. Pasolini had a certain claim on Bologna, for he had gone to high school and university there, though he hailed from the Friuli region and lived most of his adult life in Rome. In the early 1970s he was at the peak of his international fame as a filmmaker, and for many years he had been a controversial, provocative figure in Italian culture and politics. Pasolini came to fame as a poet in the late 1950s with *The Ashes of Gramsci* (*Le ceneri di Gramsci*), and its long title poem is a crucial document in postwar Italian literature. Antonio Gramsci, co-founder of the Italian Communist Party, was tried and imprisoned for many years under the Fascist regime. During his imprisonment he kept voluminous notebooks which became seminal theoretical writings on which to base a peculiarly Italian communism rooted in local needs and a locally evolved economy. During his imprisonment he also instructed fellow prisoners (some of them hard-core criminals) in literature and history. Though a child of the petite bourgeoisie—his father was a civil administrator of some kind in Sardinia—Gramsci was preoccupied with the struggles of the new industrial working classes and their place in a new communist society.

In the poem, Pasolini visits Gramsci's grave in Rome's Protestant Cemetery, where Shelley and other foreigners, mostly English, are buried. The grounds and gardens are carefully tended, and to Pasolini the place seems an image of patrician privilege. But beyond the cemetery lies the Testaccio quarter, a rough working-class slum, a *borgata*. Pasolini, child of a career military man and a schoolteacher, positions himself between the refined appointments of the burial grounds and the sordid workshops of Testaccio, between the historical imagination of Gramsci (Italian hero buried among foreigners, man of prose, strategist for the reorganization of industrial society) and the speculative imagination of Shelley (English patrician in self-imposed exile, man of poetry, visionary of revolutionized consciousness). Pasolini positions himself in the middle, isolated by his own uncertainty, "Between hope / and my old distrust," between the hope for freedom of appetite sounded out by the din of Testaccio and his old distrust of his petty bourgeois origins. Gramsci is a model of rigor in rejecting the allure of materialist culture and the exploitive relation to working-class people that capitalist culture is built on. But Pasolini, powerfully attracted sexually and ideologically to the *borgata*, also values material comforts, the remnants of the "bourgeois evils / [that] wounded my bourgeois self." (In later years, young men of the Roman *borgate* recognized the cruising Pasolini by the luxury cars he drove.) He knows that Gramsci, like so many of the foreigners buried around him, succeeded by force of will, self-discipline, and intensity of purpose, and that the workers of Testaccio survive by smarts and sweat, always a step away from chaos, tossed by momentary passions. But as a poet and intellectual living "in the non-will / of the dead postwar years," Pasolini occupies his own disconsolate, ineffectual dead zone.

To make poetry is to transform passion into a symbol world, bringing over the quick of the senses into annals of lore and image-hoarding. The intellectuality of poetry does not return a poet to the source, to the fevers of Testaccio. We take ourselves out of life in order to speak more passionately of life. Pasolini knows that his clothes, though threadbare from use, are the kind working-class people covet. He loves their vulgar taste for glamorous shopwindows with their "crude splendours" even while his own tastes force him into an ironic regard. (When he cruised the *borgate* he often changed down from his normal workaday attire to tight polyester blouses and ankle boots.) He loves the workers' hunger for life's passions in part because he has had to school himself in the formalist reflective delay so crucial to poetry. His poem is a cry at his own helplessness in the middle, that despised place, between Testaccio and the lovely gardens of death.

Pasolini never really left that middle zone, the place of contradiction. Soon after the major critical successes of *The Ashes of Gramsci* and his two novels, *A Violent Life* and *The Ragazzi*, he became an increasingly controversial filmmaker and cultural critic for major newspapers. With success came material rewards. I recognize Pasolini as the sort of artist whose political consciousness was fed by his desire to migrate to a class to which he would never in fact choose to belong. Born into the working class, he would have howled to set himself free of its system of censure and malediction. His febrile loyalties to the subproletariat of the *borgata* were conditioned by the fact that he was free to visit that life, not obligated to live it. His sexual privilege was his freedom to pick up and enjoy boys among whom he was not destined to live. But he was also an artist unafraid to suffer his contradictions and live out their consequences in public. In 1968, Pasolini published in a newspaper a poem in which he sided with the policemen then battling students during the 1968 turmoil. The police, he argued, were the children of the working class, with very limited opportunities in life. The students were, like himself, the children of the middle class and spoiled by the entitlements an unjust hierarchical society seeks to preserve and protect. The truly revolutionary gesture, the authentic Gramscian gesture, was to support the police in their conflict against the preservers of class privilege. Pasolini in effect claimed his own Marxist pedigree as justification for supporting the actions of the traditional law enforcement arm of the State.

The unmentioned presence in the poem is Keats, also buried in the Protestant Cemetery. Yeats described him as the son of a stable keeper and too much enchanted by sensuous delight. But Keats was also, perhaps most of all, the poet of the senses' disclosures. The life of forms in poetry was for him one of pure possibility and consequently a fit medium for sensuous anticipation and surprise. He may have lacked philosophy and the refinements of aristocratic intellectualism, which figures in Yeats's account of him as a boy with his nose pressed to a sweetshop window. He certainly showed his hungers, and he did not agonize over his class origins as did Pasolini, Shelley, and Yeats, for whom the passionate life was always to be found elsewhere, in the *borgata*, in a classless society, in the rooms of great houses. Middle-class contradictions are no anxiety for an artist born among the working classes. The great anxiety is to separate oneself from those origins, escaping their violent censures and intolerance for the life of the imagination. Keats's career, like D. H. Lawrence's, was a pursuit of the sensuous immediacy and hauntedness of the flesh that Pasolini anguishes over in "The Ashes of Gramsci." For Pasolini, as for so many artists of the middle class, passion becomes "problematical." (For some it becomes a high-toned dilemma; one sees poems today with ludicrous titles like "The Mind-Body Problem," "The Problem With My Heart," and "The Problem of Passion.") Artists born to the working class face their own temptations, one of which is to reduce memory and experience to mere local color or cult object. There will probably always be a sentimental market for blue-collar verities, alley cat wisdom, and tenement transcendentalism. Just as there are markets for exotic otherness, ethnic enchantments, and "subculture" opportunisms. I often remind myself not to let my work be dyed too richly or flamboyantly with Mercutio's red impetuousity—the flash of anger and impatience and want is so familiar to me. I've learned that contrariness may be the most enduring habit passed on by my working-class culture, and that its formal consequence is a barely sustained coherence of passion and idea.

3

In my twenties, I read poetry to broaden my sense of the dimensions of its mystery and ambition. The call to poetry resonated in the prose writers I was reading, Randolph Bourne, Paul Nizan, the Sartre of *The Words* and *Between Existentialism and Marxism*, Nietzsche, Ortega, and John Jay Chapman. In them I found the particular value, expressed mostly in political or moral terms, that I was pursuing in poetry: the sensuous shapeliness of form governing and measuring ungovernable passion. I felt words to be in a constant semi-solid state, however fixed and articulated their etymologies. They were not vehicles for stating passion, they were themselves the rapid uneven pulse and texture of passion. But somewhere along the way I also became persuaded, I don't know how, that the objects of the world cannot be owned by figures of consciousness. That is probably my deepest political conviction. I believe that there is in the things of the world an essential stilled singularity that cannot be expropriated even by the mastering forms of the imagination. The enchantments of representation are not true magic. Poetry does not transform the world; it embodies the particular acts and feelings of being in the world. If my ambition thrives on anything, it thrives on the way the things of the world resist words and wordiness. I love and

Pocketbook and Sauerkraut

struggle with that remoteness. The only contemporary I know who can own pieces of the world in figures of consciousness is James Merrill. (He owns pieces of the other world, too, in *The Changing Light at Sandover*.) Apart from his prodigious and well-schooled gifts as a craftsman, Merrill also has a power peculiar to the social, economic, and cultural privilege of his origins. The power and will to transform the things of the world into figures is driven by his own hunger to take and taste, as if he were the rich child who, shut away in hermetic rooms filled with images and books under the watchful eye of his nanny, had never done the rude Keatsian thing and pressed his nose to a sweetshop window.

I must have experienced poetry from the beginning—though I recollect it as a feeling only—as an attempt to fuse and discriminate at the same time, in one sentence; to blend into words the unsorted particulars of experience, and to make words not report the conflict but enact it. The figures of consciousness played out in a poem were for me not decorative or idly pleasurable but rhetorical, litigious, Mercutial, sometimes disablingly or obscurely so. (I sometimes think that working-class Roman Catholics feel the nerves of Puritanism more immediately and practically than any Protestant New Englander.) That impatience has carried over into my critical judgments. I don't like poetry with slyly built-in mechanisms of self-justification (Frost is our American master of this: equivocal wisdom born of equivocal humility), and I dislike the sentimentality of all-purpose sorrowing. I'm impatient with anyone who would define me or my work in terms of my origins. Intellectual discourse these days is full of talk about hegemonic structures or principles, and one of these is class. Begin with the determinant factor of class, the argument runs, and all other qualities and structures will follow from that. No poet can afford to think that way because it is the technique of a mind that fears the messy particulars of embodiment and believes temperament to be an accident of language rather than a part of its genetic structure.

However, though class is not determinant, it is certainly formative.

Pocketbook and Sauerkraut

When I ran my pocketbook-sauerkraut rhyme through my head or hummed "Better Buy Bird's-Eye" until its sense melted into those rhapsodic swells which Poe believed to be poetry's purest music, when I pored over the tiny reproductions of paintings in our Picture Study books in grade school or read through encyclopedia articles and poems by Poe and Millay and Lindsay at the free library, they were not a richness beyond my poverty (we were not poor, we simply had no money, and there were no books in our house) or a promise of transport beyond my means. They were enchanting forms, mysterious shapes, which had a density of ordered feeling of which life itself seemed a rough sketch or study. My own day-to-day life felt like constant bad weather inside my head, of anger and sullenness, hilarity and melancholy, with no placid middle zones, just as there seemed to be no middle temperaments among the boys I played with, who were either predatory, coarse, manipulative, and crazy, or else quiet, nervous, anxious to please, and in jeopardy. In time, the poetry I aspired to write would be one without middle zones, without a sustained discursive middle range or plain presentational balance. I knew I did not want to sound like Tennyson, sonorous, dignified, and responsible. Browning was closer to what I wanted, capable of the most exquisite lyric effects but also twitchy and volatile and impatient. I am touched by Henry James's description of Browning reading his poems aloud in a way that suggested he hated them, biting and twisting the words, anxious, unsatisfied, inflamed by their very existence. And I still feel an opaque sympathy with the character of Lippo Lippi, a sympathy grounded in my class origins, which sharpened my sense of the otherness of the things of the world and somehow encouraged that sense to become a formal desire. Lippi makes a string of pictures of the world because it is so apart from him and he knows he could be engulfed in the oblivion of that otherness.

People in my neighborhood were scrupulously honest with one another and with local storekeepers, but the men felt little guilt pinching things from their workplace. My first writing materials—it sounds grandiose to call them that—were hot goods. Like many children, I scribbled away at stories and plays. The miserable wage my father earned at Temple University Hospital was offset by the availability of small items from a friend of his in Supplies. Most of my father's co-workers took advantage, too, and like him most had gone to work straight out of grade school or after a year or two of high school. Bolts of colored twine, paper clips, staples, grease pencils, lead pencils, index cards, scratch pads and legal pads and letter files—portable things easily smuggled home but, in a household like ours, almost completely useless. Paper clips to attach what to what? We had no "documents," kept no records, wrote and received no letters, never made shopping lists. The stationery was a strange "bonus," a little windfall that brought no real benefit because it answered no real need. Except mine, which was secret. I now had materials. I still do. To go with the gleaming Ticonderoga pencils, my father sneaked home a crank sharpener, now attached to one of my bookcases, and a hyena-shaped Swingline stapler that I still use. A few years ago, long after his death, on a visit home I rooted through some boxes in the cellar and found remnants of my childhood stash, and I've put them to use, the lacquered yellow pencils asleep in their slipboxes, the legal pads warped and browned at the edges, and the grease pencils with their beautiful sharp pullstring coils. A fair amount of what I've written over the years has been done on hot stuff, stolen materials that were, in the conscience of my people, worker's compensation.

Poetry in Common

First you see the headdresses, tall colorful *tablitas* decorated with painted clouds and phallic shapes, rising from the ceremonial chamber at the edge of the mesa. Then the dancers, the masked kachinas, fifty of them walking single file through the village into the plaza, their steps sounded by turtleshell rattles, while an elder calls out prayers and commands. Among them are twelve masked "lady kachinas," men dressed as the sisters and relatives of the masked spirits. Thus begins the Niman, or Home Dance, when kachinas bring to Hopi villages the fruits of harvest—corn, melon, squash—then depart for their home in the San Francisco Mountains to spend the next few months praying for rain. Their line dance is patterned on the four-sided shape of the plaza, itself patterned on the four corners of the world and the four-world historical cycle the Hopi have lived through. They repeat the dance three times, at different points on the plaza, never allowing the line to close into a circle, since this Fourth World, our own, is imperfect, still moving toward balanced completion. After the dancing, the kachinas file back to the ceremonial chamber, past basketball hoops, TV antennas, listing plywood privies, half-finished or abandoned dwellings of unfaced cinder block, and the dust spurs of cars and pick-ups.

The Hopi villages in Arizona constitute one of the most hermetic communities in North America. The reservation is governed by the Tribal Council, and each village is for the most part a self-contained polity. Government, the orderly pursuit and maintaining of communal good, is conducted according to the balanced relation between material contingency and spiritual necessity. Physically, the older villages of

Shingopovi, Walpi, and Old Oraibi, high on their mesas, look as much like autonomous political entities as any walled Renaissance city state. Clan structure and religious observance regulate most aspects of traditional life. From them radiates a network of social and cultural relations grounded in reciprocities, balances, secrecies, and initiatory disclosures that make the Hopi seem not just a unified culture but a coherent society.

The oral poetry of Hopi prayers, chants, and stories is fused to political observance, political insofar as the social collective can cohere, can keep from going crazy, only if the rituals are observed. Poetry such as the elder's cries during the Home Dance expresses the history of the people as systems of vigilance, assistance, and obedience. The poetry does not contain history in Pound's sense of an epic as a poem containing history. Nor is it recitation. Hopi poetry, like that of many Native American cultures, is reenactment or recapitulation of the past, of the knowledge a people has of its own reality and destiny. Poetry reminds the listener-spectators that they are the People. It is not the reality of a perfect society—for years traditionalists and friendlies have bitterly disputed the issue of self-determination—and it does not esteem originality or idiosyncratic expression.

Kachina is the essence of the culture. As actual presences, kachinas are companions, helpers, censors, parental enforcers, dramatic personas, intercessors, and Hermetic crossers from sky to earth. Kachina is also a spiritual quality that constitutes a politics, for it is reason and sanction of order in the plaza, in the public space where separate private lives and troubles may convene and perhaps be healed. The vitality of that power is passed on like lore from one generation to another. The ogre kachina that suddenly shows up one night to scare and chastise a disrespectful child will appear a few years later at that child's secret initiation and reveal himself as Uncle Louie. If the spirit world is profaned or insulted, the material organization of the political order also suffers.

I don't want to idealize Hopi culture. I want to acknowledge it as one piece of a United States that even Whitman, in all his glee for diversity, could not have imagined. I want to say that Hopi culture exists in and of and apart from North American life, and that a poet who chooses to write about political feeling is decisively shaped by the recognition of that separateness, and of the separateness of so many other political and cultural entities. These separatenesses create the turbulence that is American political awareness. As descendants of immigrant populations from Europe, Asia, Latin America, and other places, many of us may admire or covet the apparent stability of Hopi society, at the same time recognizing that it exists as a racially homogeneous, small, aloof, self-contained, and self-defining group. As a race of Americans, we know ourselves as bunches of *others*, an unstable compound of different bloods, races, and religions working often with forbearing tolerance and just as often with violent despair on the project of a coherent American polity.

That project lives as an image of visionary possibility in the American imagination. It is elemented by the Hopi ("subdued" in the 1800s by a troop of Negro cavalry dispatched from Washington), by traditional societies like the Zuñi and Navajo, and by the Rio Grande Pueblo people who, after hearing Mass on a feast day, perform corn dances in the plaza while an elder goes house to house sprinkling cornmeal on the stove, the TV set, and the heads of children and of Baby Jesus statuettes. Elemented, too, by the peoples of Brooklyn's Crown Heights where months ago first and second generation Islanders were fighting in the streets with the Lubavitcher Hasidim over the death of a black child run over by a car in the Grand Rebbe's entourage. New York's mayor, an African American, was completely ineffectual in mediating the conflict. A few days later, in Philadelphia, an eighteen-year-old boy named Reilly was stabbed to death by a Southeast Asian boy, while in Louisiana a former Grand Wizard of the Ku Klux Klan, having nearly been elected Governor, declared he would run for the Presidency. These tabloid facts are inflammatory signs of the divisive strains that must be dealt with by poets concerned with the polity, who begin with a recognition of conflicted differentness and convulsive unlikeness.

Poetry in Common

We lack what Hannah Arendt calls a common world, a public space that makes possible and sustains speech about differentness shared in common. It can be an actual place—agora, plaza, town hall—or a faculty of language. It has the power "to gather [people] together, to relate and to separate them." It calls us together even while it prevents us from falling over one another. Modern mass society, Arendt argues, has lost the power to assemble and separate as one action. Obviously the common world of the Greek polis is not available to us. We are either falling all over ourselves, physically and linguistically, or we are passionately dismantling the common into sectarian orthodoxies and ideologies. As a founding place for poets, the United States is farther from a common world than any other modern industrial society, though our most tenacious covering fiction is the unity of differentness, a thousand voices speaking at once to make a common intelligible song. A poet's voice has to be one of those, but the poet's work is also to contrive a signature form-language distinct from that great noise.

The important political activity of poetry is to approach a common world by exercising the contentious, even divisive, energies of the idiosyncratic imagination. It is a singular, cranky consciousness that can yet absorb and propagate the normative consciousness of the many. If any poet's speech is talk formalized, a political poet's speech is dissenting talk about a common world. "The world is not humane just because it is made by human beings," Arendt writes. "And it does not become humane just because the human voice sounds in it, but only when it has become the object of discourse . . . . We humanize what is going on in the world and in ourselves only by speaking of it, and in the course of speaking of it we learn to be human." When a poet says *we*, however, it is dyed with possibility and with the accumulated distortions and inflections of historical knowledge, irony, passionate commitment to artifice, and the constant critical play of the plasticity of language, even while Arendt's normative *we* lies folded somewhere, somehow, active in the poet's sensibility.

The American imagination may feel that a common world exists among the Hopi, but it also knows such a world to be one remote, exclusionary element in the turbulent process of differentiation and inclusion which is the North American project. A poet's political work is to make images of that project. I don't mean image in Pound's sense, as an intellectual and emotional complex in an instant of time, as a configuration within a poem, but rather the poem itself taken as an image, as paintings or photographs are images, a patterned expressive entirety. The formal passion is the passion for relatedness. But our defining trait is divisiveness, separateness, spiritual vastation, individual grievance elevated to general grief, exasperating variety heaving tumultuously now and again into exasperating uniformity.

I would separate poetry of political concern from the kind of political poetry I'm trying to define. "Political" is not an emphasis or characteristic, and it does not apply to poems in which *we* is merely the sign of sentimental opportunism or genteel magnanimity. Political poetry, if it is to be of use, does not preach to the converted or contrive positions certain of an audience's approval. It is not a condition of excited nerves strummed by historical occasion or a migratory action of social concern, though it will often have these in its genetic material. The intensest political poetry volatilizes issue or event in the image-event of the poem, in the formalizing and often distorting fires of poetic speech. When Pound rips into the specific occurrences of usury in Cantos XII and XIV, it's a corrective rage aimed at a way of mind that out of commercial self-interest deforms the natural relation between labor and its products, between natural abundance and human wealth. Pound's real subject is that relation.

What do we sing? If poetry is language grounded in ordinary usage and the supple happenstance of the commonplace that must also enact the extremest densities of consciousness—densities sometimes so etherealized that they seem a kind of air ore—how does a poet tell the experience of being a singular self blended into an undifferentiated crowd of others? There is of course the way of witness: to render accurate accounts of what occurs, to acknowledge the evidence of the human. The denunciation of atrocity is an act of sympathetic magic, that by speaking of what human beings can do to one another we clarify and restore to ourselves the knowledge of evil so that we might be more alert to its presence. It was Pound, manic archivist and history-broadcaster, who lectured poets on the need to make accurate reports (though his own judgment in such matters was at times contemptible). Another way, the one that concerns me more, includes witness in the making of a more responsive image of relatedness. It is the way of poetry that admits not only the quick of events but also meditative lyric analysis—excited, rude, self-conscious and subdued and uncongenial, with wilder sorts of hilarity, rage, forgiveness, and compassion running loose in the tonality. It is a poetry willing to offend when syntax upsets the equilibrium of judicious deliberation, when hot feeling turns a "clear political position" into a sticky fever dream.

In all this Whitman, as in too much else, spoke first. His boisterous *we* was summons and deposition. His superb announcement that he contained multitudes was the monstrous measure against which poets have since defined their own singular place in a crowd. But for all his healthymindedness about the new Union and its democratic ethos, Whitman was haunted by what he called in *Democratic Vistas* "the fear of conflicting and irreconcilable interiors, and the lack of a common skeleton." The healing agent for this condition was religion, by which he seemed to mean a general spiritual consistency running through the populace, an ad hoc way of melting down differences and conflicting interests into one undifferentiated essence: "At the core of democracy, finally, is the religious element. All the religions, old and new, are there."

They are still there, and they still haven't fused into one element. Whitman had an Adamic talent for declaring the terms of a crisis without actually seeing it. He prophesied what his successors would confront, that in a democracy individualism ("which isolates") would conflict with "the adhesiveness of love, that fuses, ties and aggregates, making the races comrades, and fraternizing all." The conflict would be pacified by religion, "breathing into the proud, material tissue, the breath of life." But whose religion? Surely not a politician's all-purpose opportunistic Christianity, or the religions practiced on Indian reservations, in Harlem mosques and churches, in the temples of the Lubavitcher, or at Quaker meetings. I understand Whitman's aching faith in the unity of a nation whose wounded he lovingly nursed during the Civil War, but I also wish he had squared up against the facts and ethical consequences of the 1863 racist draft riots in New York. A poetry of American political feeling restores to us the persuasion that we always seem to be starting afresh though, ragged and fatigued with history and the consequences of diversity, we don't feel fresh at all.

Public Music

As early as 1913, in his essay "Patria Mia," Ezra Pound affirmed that a work of art does not have to contain "any statement of a political . . . conviction, but it nearly always implies one." He had begun writing the *Cantos* around 1904, adapting epic form to suit his own ends, not only to give passionate intelligible shape to political conviction but also to dramatize the movements of a mind holding such conviction. His view of an epic as "a poem containing history" has obvious precedents in antiquity, but we should not presume too much continuity with the past. Mycenean civilization, the source of the Homeric poems, recorded and preserved its traditions, its identity, and consequently its political coherence and stability through the oral transmission from generation to generation of facts and myths recited in the rhythmic orders of verse. Poetry was essentially encyclopedic, archival, conservative. It constituted a shelf of reference works on astronomy, medicine, social convention, and religion, and therefore contributed crucially to the knowledge needed to preserve and improve the social order. The Mycenean palace complex and the Greek polis that evolved from it, Eric Havelock tells us in *A Preface to Plato,* used poetry as an unofficial table of contents of the tribe. Without the oral practice they called poetry the early polis could not have survived. Poetry from the archaic period to around the sixth century was not literature with a political theme or element, and it was unimaginably far from the prerogatives of self-expression we now take for granted. Poetry was instead a political necessity.

The encyclopedic didactic procedures of the *Cantos* convince me that Pound wanted his poem to be a political stabilizer just as poetry had been in antiquity. He takes over prose documents like Adams's letters to recover and conserve the process of judicious deliberation just as oral performers once preserved the protocols of tribal oratory that we hear in the *Iliad*. Pound's epic boils over with quoted testimony, cited documents, a carnival of raised voices installed in wisdom booths. As the log of a journey into knowledge, which Pound called periplum ("not as land looks on a map / but as sea bord seen by men sailing"), the poem is an idiosyncratic Modernist *paideia*, a system and log of developmental learning. Its instructiveness is irritatingly present, although the instruction is aimed as intently at the poet himself as it is at us. The poem is meant *at least* to demonstrate what a person needs to know to be an informed responsible world citizen. The amassed slabs of erudition serve this end, and even the lyric passages so often singled out for their beauty are usually encoded in some kind of historicized speech, whether it derives from Tyndale's translations of scripture, the Edwardian mannerisms of Pound's youth, or the Anglo-Saxon and troubadour idioms Pound contrived in his translation work. Much of the *Cantos* is as antiqued, as artificially pitched, as anything in *The Fairie Queen*, but for different purposes. It's not a recovered or idealized diction that Pound wants, but a tone and idiom of pastness conserved as a guide to Good Mind. The antiqued idioms are, in any event, hammered, chopped, cut up, collaged, and rorschached into the emergent periplum patterns of the poem. Pound knew that the poem's manner as well as its matter would play a role in determining our own *paideuma*, which he glossed (out of Frobenius) as "the mental formation, the inherited habits of thought, the conditionings, aptitudes of a given race or time." The spastic turns of attention, the long ribbons of information unfurled in the cantos treating Adams, Van Buren, Chinese history, and monetary theory, the eruptions of religious feelings and sacred visions, the flashing voices (we hear Chinese emperors, arms manufacturers, writers and philosophers, American presidents, the guards and detainees at Pisa, the poet's wife and child and neighbors, and on and on) all combine to make a private store of memory into a public archive. The *Cantos* may not be a political necessity as poetry was thought to be in antiquity, but its formal plying of fact and vision insists on the essential relation between the political order and the poetic imagination.

Pound was Dante's pupil most in his understanding that formal invention is exercise and expression of political sense. Unlike Dante's lengths of processional narrative, however, Pound's formal means are congestive, incremental, and reiterative, all utterance so much on a level, so apparently nonhierarchical, that what readers like myself experience as a tedium of warehoused facts and collaged stories may also be a democratic delirium of statement. The formal ideal for Pound, I suppose, was to say everything at once yet have every thing said distinct. But I also feel the poet acting as an all-gathering and willful governor of that incipient chaos; Pound's vigor of address and headstrong assertions are instances of what he called *directio voluntatis*.

The opening of Canto 38 is representative of this method. The epigraph is Dante's denunciation of Philip the Fair for debasing coinage to finance a military campaign:

> *il duol che sopra Senna*
> *Induce, falseggiando la moneta.*
> —*Paradiso* 19:118

An' that year Metevsky went over to America del Sud
    (and the Pope's manners were so like Mr. Joyce's,
      got that way in the Vatican, weren't like that before)
    Marconi knelt in the ancient manner
      like Jimmy Walker sayin' his prayers.
His Holiness expressed a polite curiosity
    as to how His Excellency had chased those
electric shakes through the a'mosphere.
    Lucrezia
Wanted a rabbit's foot,

Public Music

27

and he, Metevsky said to the one side
(three children, five abortions and died of the last)
    he said: the other boys got more munitions
(thus cigar-makers whose work is highly repetitive
can perform the necessary operations almost automatically
and at the same time listen to readers who are hired
for the purpose of providing mental entertainment while they
work; Dexter Kimball 1929.)

The lines stack facts that bleed and seep one into another. The money-for-arms content of the epigraph keys in Metevsky, Pound's name for Sir Basil Zaharoff, a successful arms merchant early in the century whose capitalist power suggests other orders of power, embodied in two of Pound's personal acquaintances, Pope Pius XI (whom Pound knew before his ascendency) and James Joyce. He then layers in a man of science and technology, Guglielmo Marconi, whose piety is shared by a most unlikely match, the American politico Jimmy Walker. (But no more unlikely a match than the Pontiff and Joyce.) Pound crosshatches the associations even more thickly when he remembers Lucrezia Borgia's superstitiousness, verging on religiosity, and suggests that her rabbits where like those "electric shakes" Marconi (inventor of the wireless telegraph) chased through the atmosphere and which so amazed the Pontiff. The mention of skyborne power returns Pound's attention to Metevsky and the guns-and-bombs industry which, he concludes, can be made even more efficient by borrowing the labor techniques Dexter Kimball introduced to the rollers of big cigars, fusing capitalist productivity with droning mental enchantments.

The idioms race from poky vernacular to mock ceremonial to prosy hum. The lines storm with gossip. The data, flooding the poet's consciousness, suggest the menacing fluidity and indiscriminate massiveness of that salient force in modern politics: the crowd. Pound is not so much interested in differentiating the facts as he is in similitudes,

Public Music

match-ups, correspondences, the associative orders by which he can hold in a simultaneity of occurrence the dazzling heterogeneous instants of his experience. (This way of making political poetry is also the mechanics of paranoia.) He even suggests allegorical equivalences between men and professional activity: Metevsky = Commerce; Pius XI = Organized Religion; Joyce = Art; Marconi = Science; Walker = Ward Politics; Kimball = Labor Technology. That, at any rate, may be the formal pattern, though it's not the way I actually experience the poetry. Pound tumbles personal anecdote with the historical record in such a way as to make me feel I'm coming into an awareness of something that may at any moment, now or later in the poem, be radically revised or fragmented. The log of the coastline journey gets bulkier as the work progresses, and its entries become more obsessive and bullying. One of them is announced in the epigraph above: the use of money.

Canto 38 dates from the early 1930s, by which time Pound was convinced that the proper use of money was a determining factor in the civil order and therefore determinant in the intellectual, moral, and artistic orders. He believed that the expressions of the soul of an age in its painting, sculpture, music, and writing were exact indicators of political balance. And that balance was determined by the degree to which money functioned as evidence and extension of natural abundance. Money is "a ticket for the orderly distribution of WHAT IS AVAILABLE . . . . it is NOT in itself abundance." Usura, strictly speaking, was the practice of renting money; generally, it was any use of money that violated the appropriation of natural abundance for moderate, necessary human use. Given Pound's view of paideuma as the interrelatedness of all values and actions in a culture, he believed that usura inevitably shaped the products of consciousness. He could read the process of usura in the history of art. In 1938, he explained to his Italian translator what he meant by the phrase in Canto 45, "with usura the line grows thick": "means the line in painting and design. Quattrocento painters are still in morally clean era when usury and buggery were on a par. As the moral sense becomes . . . incapable of moral distinction . . . painting gets bitched. I can tell the bank-rate and component of tolerance for usury in any epoch by the quality of *line* in a painting." Pound always preferred the Italian Primitives and Florentine painting to the mess-of-shadows colorism of later Venetian and Baroque art. He put his preference into practice. The *Cantos* is a poem of perspective manipulations, vectors, cross-hatchings, the allegorical clarities of good *disegno*. His remarks make clear that he believed style was political expressiveness, and that politics grounded in usura, in the unnatural exploitative creation and circulation of money, violates Good Mind.

I read the *Cantos* as an image of economy. The natural wealth of learning in the poem is presented as an active, patterning exemplum of complete consciousness, which in an instant can connect a corn kernel to a commodity exchange to a supper to an ear-shaped sculptural form to the slow presence of Demeter among us. The poem insists on related-ness and on the political need to constantly review and adjudicate relat-edness. In this respect it's a political instrument. I mean an instrument for political effect, for Pound saw how in the modern period the intent of bankers, industrialists, politicians, and of certain intellectuals, artists, and impresarios, has been to break down the consciousness of related-ness. Specialization, isolation, "individual initiative," and special inter-ests distract a populace from an awareness of patterns that connect nat-ural abundance and labor to the processes of work and the circulation of money. Pound detested abstraction because it estranges us from the actuality of shared destiny. *Usura*—abstraction generally—could thus set human action at vicious odds with nature. It's grotesquely apt, there-fore, that Pound's most vicious error was in abstracting race from indi-viduals, the Jew from Jews, and worse, to do so in service to another abstraction: Authority.

Pound loved the roughneck improvisations and rakehell moodiness of the American character. I often think he loved especially what he could never get quite right, the dialectical and regional colorism of

American speech. (His celebrated "great ear" was mostly a bookworm's literary contrivance, not the great ear of someone who listens to what's actually said.) His intellectual formations and predilections, however, were elitist, hierarchical, and sectarian, from the Gnostic Cathar brotherhood and the teachings of Kung, to the money policies of C.H. Douglas and the initiation rites of Eleusis. His apparently egalitarian all-at-once style was rooted in, and often takes as its subject, the pedagogical hierarchy of master and pupil, adept and neophyte. As a poet of wanton intellectual appetites he welcomed heterogeneity, but as a political thinker within his poetry he was wary of the instabilities created by a contentious, racially pied, inarticulate populace. His mixed attitudes toward authority are a source of unrest throughout the *Cantos*. While he sought in some ways to undermine established authority—by criticizing the efficacy of capitalist economies, by advocating a complete overhaul of money policies, by insisting on the actual presence of deities in the material world—the poem itself stands as a directory of authority and masteries.

Most of the raw experience in the *Cantos* is fippled by magisterial texts. In 1911 Pound described his procedure as "the method of luminous detail . . . certain facts give one a sudden insight into circumjacent conditions, into their causes, their effects, into sequence and law." The luminous details come as often from source material as from Pound's invention: from the Jefferson-Adams correspondence, Confucian analects, Malatesta's mailbag, Martin Van Buren's autobiography; and from translations of translations, of Divus's Latin version of the *nekuia* from the *Odyssey*, for instance, and of French versions of Chinese documents. Even gossip, the fabulous gossip that rushes in and out of the poem, is a patterning of authority. Pound reports Yeats's report of Beardsley's deathbed remark, "Beauty is difficult," to defend his own stylistic adventures in the *Cantos*. Pound's admiration for Dante has always been apparent. More important is what he refused, or what the age (and the kind of art it necessitated) refused him. The *Comedy* has serial, lucid, conclusive confrontations between the pilgrim and his instructors. The *Cantos*, however, is mostly second- or third-hand transmission; the passion of confrontational engagement so consistent in Dante's poem is deflected, baffled, and rechanneled by mediating authorities, intervening texts. The result is not a processional interrogation of the history of a consciousness but an encyclopedist fever dream.

Pound's judgments of historical figures were often based on homologies. He came to a late appreciation of the Italian reformer Mazzini when he perceived in Mazzini theories of social credit later advocated by Douglas. He was similarly impressed by something in Mazzini's character that he admired in other powerful figures: *directio voluntatis*. Around 1941 Pound writes: "What counts is the direction of the will." He saw the same quality in Italian Fascism: "The name of the Fascist era is *Voluntas*." The directed will is the destiny-forging element in the *Comedy*, wherein sinfulness is the act of directing the will toward an inappropriate object or allowing the will to be deflected from the good, proper object. Sin is not so much a bad act as it is a wrong way. *Directio voluntatis* can decide the fate of an individual or of a populace or nation. Dante describes it in *De Vulgari Eloquentia* as the opposite of *abuleia*, paralysis of the will, a condition Pound detested. (That Pound, a declared non-Christian, should take over and adapt to his own purposes a Christian, indeed Thomistic, moral philosophy is one of the many kinds of intellectual colonizing perpetrated in the *Cantos*.) Pound was convinced that Mussolini would be remembered for his personal *voluntas* and his passion for order: "The Duce will stand not with despots and the lovers of power but with the lovers of ORDER." Pound's sense of good order, derived from Confucius, is set out early in the famous lines of Canto 13: "If a man have not order within him / He can not spread order about him; / And if a man have not order within him / His family will not act with due order; / And if the prince have not order within him / He can not put order in his dominions."

Pound was so intent on instructing us in the ideal polity of the mind, himself acting (as he felt, I think, historically obligated to do) as master teacher, that he ignored particular occurrences. In the interests of order Mussolini imprisoned or confined many of the best, most independent minds of his time, Gramsci being the most conspicuous and tragic instance. Cesare Pavese and Carlo Levi were, along with many other writers and artists, banished to the south and put under house arrest, and politically aloof poets like Eugenio Montale lost their jobs for refusing to join the party. Pound may have been unaware of these events, but he was not unaware of the derangements of order that artists often incite by challenging the normalcies and niceties of established values. Formally at least he was doing just that in the *Cantos*, even while the poem in part argues for the importance of political order under strong leaders. The poem would be politically less volatile, however, if it were mostly a brief for steely hierarchy sustained by *voluntas*. But the *Cantos* also argues that a renewed vision of wholeness requires incoherence, confusion, and obscured destinies, and that the process of defining a polity shares the dissonance and chaos and indefiniteness that goes into the making of art: "Wilderness of renewals, confusion / Basis of renewals, subsistence, / Glazed green of the jungle." Essential to the wilderness and to the renewals is a vision of sacred presence in the world.

In the *Cantos*, especially in the Pisan sequence and the agonizing meditations of the final drafts and fragments, gods and goddesses— Pound believed most passionately in Aphrodite and Dionysus/Zagreus: intoxicators, chaos-bringers, sweeteners of sense, light-bearers, leaders, disturbers of good order—materialize as data of consciousness pulled into the poem with all the particularity and abrupt selective decisiveness of the contents of Sigismundo's mail pouch. Though for long stretches of the poem we are allowed to forget it, Pound's political thinking was inseparable from his Neoplatonic religious vision. In secular terms the directed will of a populace, governed by leaders with a sense of order, can make for a balanced state. This can succeed, though, only if grounded in a vision of human origins, and Pound's vision was that

Athenian one which held that we are children of the earth, and that earth may be our paradise: "the forms of men rose out of *gaia* / Le Paradis n'est pas artificiel." Human intellect refracts divine intelligence, which is itself embodied or embedded in the things of the world, in the materiality of the eucalyptus pip he pocketed on his way to the Disciplinary Training Center in 1944, in the visionary forms of Dread Aphrodite that he sees from his prison cage at Pisa, and in the moth of smoke rising from his smoke hole.

This Neoplatonic way of regarding the physical world takes shape fairly early in the poem, where it is already associated with government and the artist's place in the polity: "Forms, forms and renewal, god held in the air, / Form seen, and then clearness, / Bright void, without image." This comes in the midst of Canto 25's narrative of the history of Venetian government and the disputed contract for Titian's decorations of the Doge's palace in the early 1550s. Very late in the poem, in Canto 113, Pound says "there is something intelligent in the cherrystone," a principle of order, but principle in process of growth and change, articulated in material presence. These are instances when the poet's imagination holds the world's harmonious order, its spirit and matter, in a pattern of words. There are other instances when I want to shake the poem and, taking up its own methods, instruct *it*: that the gods may also appear to human beings whose obsession with control and order, guided by *directio voluntatis*, might lead to genocide or the tolerance or calculated ignorance thereof; and that no complete political vision, no actual political wholeness, can be founded on selective or edited relatedness. Pound's own viciousness converged on his spurious distinction between the big Jew (banker, usurer types like Rothschild) and the little Jew (like, presumably, Zukofsky and Oppen). He would have us believe, and would have himself believe, that he nursed murderous hatred toward the abstract Jew but not toward real, ordinary, artistic sorts of Jews. This is not an example of temperament fouling intelligence, but of the desire for a deliberate, discriminating purity, borne along by rhapsodic authority, contaminating the possibility for a useful, practical whole community made up of real human beings.

Pound finally situated his imagined world, his politically whole earthly paradise, "between KUNG and ELEUSIS," between a balanced civil order constellated around familial and social order as articulated by Confucius, and the secret, exclusionary, initiatory, transformational, ecstatic mystery religion where the gods are airborne presences materialized in the things of the world: "That butterfly has gone out thru my smoke hole." Deity does not sponsor the world of things, it floods and saturates it and is the ordinary visionary aspect by which relations are seen. In the last fragmentary chunks of the poem the political is clearly inseparable from spiritual relatedness and continuity. There are moments when Pound's vision quest is achieved, when he *saw*:

> And for one beautiful day there was peace.
> Brancusi's bird
> > in the hollow of pine trunks
> or when the snow was like sea foam

His aspiration "To make a church / or an altar to Zagreus" remains with him. Pound conceived of his work, however, not as prophecy but as agency, voluntas operating through the forms of art. When at the end he declares in sorrow "that I lost my center / fighting the world. / The dreams clash / and are shattered— / and that I tried to make a paradiso / terrestre," he's announcing the failure of his attempt, not the inadequacy of the vision. Pursuing the vision of wholeness, he lost his way by becoming snared in the very confusion his poem presents as a matrix for renewals.

In his book *Illusion and Reality*, the 1930s Marxist writer Christopher Caudwell describes the fantasy element in the harvest dance of native peoples. The dancers' objective, the harvest, does not yet exist; it lives only in the imagination of the participants. "The violence of the dance, the screams of the music and hypnotic rhythm of the verse," Caudwell says, alienate the dancers from the present moment and expand their consciousness to include the fantasy harvest image as something present. That world, in the frenzy of the dance, becomes real. When the dance is over that object stays fixed in the mind as a sustaining purpose so that the tribe can make the fantastic harvest a reality. Though Caudwell does not pursue this, it seems to me that in poetry the instinctual claims of cadence, diction, sonority, repetition, rhythm, and emergent spectral structure are equivalent to the singing and pulse of the harvest dance. In formal terms these powers or "primitive elements" create an image, a fantasy image, of a political reality. A poem's blood powers and formal appetites create an imaginative pattern—that is, an image—which is as essential to its political content as any statement the poem makes. Indeed, when these powers are interdicted or suppressed or censored by the poet's desire to make statements that are unimpeachable, correct, or opportunistic, the poem turns into propaganda, which requires a puritanical curtailment of the hunger for invention. The imagination in pursuit of political vision has to follow its own unstable ways, must sometimes be caught up in impolitic concerns and headstrong formal impulses. No modern poet can produce the equivalent of harvest dance music. Our shared public music is fated to be idiosyncratic in origin, and our vision one not of fixed tribal relations but of the process of relatedness.

Poetry can, of course, be a form of political activism, or a sign of it, a cry, a shout, the voice raised on or against occasion. But that does not make it political in the sense I'm after here, as a constant inquiry into relatedness, as the torment of affects and sympathies induced by concern for the destiny of the polity—which is the destiny of a structure as well as of the human beings who define, inhabit, and realize the structure. To cry out against atrocity, against any outrage to our shared sense of the good, is one of poetry's most important offices. What we find in a poet like George Oppen, however, is that sort of cry muffled, broken

up, and transmuted into an intensely personal inquisitiveness, an inter-
rogating regard for the relation of the individual to the human collec-
tive. For him it is finally a question of an ethic, one in which moral value
is grounded in an awareness of the destiny of the species.

Oppen once tried to explain to Hugh Kenner the reasons for the
long silence that followed his first book of poems, *Discrete Series*. Kenner
interrupted, "In brief, it took twenty-five years to write the next poem."
Oppen relished the story and retold it many times, not because of the
hard differences in the two men's political views but because Kenner's
remark really does account for the break between Oppen's political and
poetic activity. He was not abandoning poetry, he was setting it aside
until he learned things he felt he needed to learn. He did not believe in
political poetry. "If you decide to do something politically," he insisted,
"you do something that has political efficacy." And so, beginning in the
mid-1930s he spent more than twenty years in political activity, first
helping the poor and dispossessed during the Great Depression, then
working as a communist party organizer. After serving in World War II
he fled to Mexico (in 1950) to escape harassment by the McCarthy
committee. He began writing poetry again in 1958.

The book that marked his return, *The Materials*, bore an epigraph
from Maritain's *Creative Intuition and the Art of Poetry*: "We awake in the
same moment to ourselves and to things." Such waking is a pure Objec-
tivist moment, when consciousness cleanses perception and objectifies
its subjects. It's also a moment of pure relatedness. The notion of "the
Things" is very important for Maritain. They are the elements that make
up the world that the poet both inhabits and confronts; they are "that
infinite host of beings, aspects, events, physical and moral tangles of
horror and beauty." The Things, moreover, possess the chaotic force of
feeling that an artist experiences, "the feelings of primitive men looking
at the all-pervading force of Nature, or of the old Ionian philosophers
saying that 'all things are full of gods.'" This is a description of radical
imaginative sympathy, when the poet finds himself or herself a con-

sciousness apart from the Things *and* dispersed among them. Oppen told that experience as an act of witness: "What I've seen / Is all I've found: myself."

A poet's intelligence feeds on the desire for analogue, correspondence, and likeness, even when such desire distracts from political actuality. Metaphor can be frivolous diversion or mere illustration. But the search for correspondence is, or should be, a search for wholeness, an imagined restoration of completeness. To the eye of Ezra Pound, imprisoned in the Disciplinary Training Center in Pisa, the mountain he sees nearby is in likeness of the holy mountain of Taishan in China, and both are in likeness of Mount Chocuroa in New Hampshire, which was a favorite place for William James, who meditated there on the divided soul of Americans who must choose between Europe and America. Metaphor may seditiously set the mind against itself, or it may promise a new order and unity. Oppen's great theme is naturally his most political: the singular and the numerous—the one in and of (or against) the many. Likeness is both vehicle and tenor of his theme. In "Population" the numerous is represented by the conceivable but unimaginable expanse of the sea. (A seadog all his life, Oppen spoke of these things with real expertise.) The singular mind coming into awareness is born not to a true solitude but to a tenacious conviction of its solitude: "Like a flat sea, / Here is where we are, the empty reaches / Empty of ourselves." It is that *we*, the collective, which already releases what the poet in his sincerity must acknowledge; at the same time that the mind "born/ alone to ocean" feels itself a solitude, it is, *we* are, a mass, a crowd, "the moment's / Populace sea-borne and violent."

Consciousness generates likenesses of its own structure and functions. The mind is a mansion, a data base, a machine or cyberspace or wilderness. Part of the work of poetry is to reveal or invent (only to then question and correct or demolish) such models. We allow them, for a while anyway, to shape our vision of ourselves, our capacities and destiny. The title of one of Oppen's poems, "The Crowded Countries of the Bomb," is a rubric for this situation. The image the title composes could not have existed before the invention of nuclear firepower, though Oppen is also drawing on the knowledge that bombs generally, their shape and sound and effects, live in the modern imagination as deeply and as ordinarily as helmets and swords lived in the minds of Homeric singers. The poem suggests that one new model for public space, for the space of politics, is the shelter; not a fallout shelter (or not only that) but the shield created by chance—almighty chance that, "as if a god," has so far spared our species from nuclear annihilation. Oppen wants a name for this place we have entered: "Despair? Ourselves?" The country of the bomb is, by his reckoning, the country of ourselves, the shelter made "of each other's backs and shoulders / Entering the country that is / Impenetrably ours." The new thing in the world, the nuclear bomb, forces us to revise all our previous mental images of human community. The new country is impenetrably ours because although we ourselves element it, it's a shelter we cannot in fact enter, for it is finally no shelter at all from what we ourselves have made. We might just as well try to ward off disease by hiding inside our bodies. The poem is not grim soothsaying. Oppen does not go in for prophecy. His poem is rather an inquiry into newly fashioned likeness, a provisional definition of the generations, of the more-than-one. Like so much of Oppen's work, it seems nearly toneless, though I never feel it's aloof or noncommittal. The music it makes is that of a mind scrutinizing its own imaginings and the source of those imaginings in the changing Things.

Anecdote is an instrument of political vision. Oppen's experience of conscience, played out from the 1930s to the 1950s (later, too, in his witness of events in the 1960s), lives in his poems but is not displayed as a glamor-object. His own sort of heroical will has the appearance and tone of diffidence, of witness-as-forbearance. He doesn't announce the vividness of his experience or proclaim its privileges; he simply writes poems that express its knowledge, nowhere more intensely than in "Of Being Numerous," where words and their political values are tested against the public space. Language needs a public space where words like "the fortunate" and "the People" will have shared meaning and sense. The modern city, however, is built of "walled avenues / In which one cannot speak." It's not for lack of an agora, but rather that the entire city has become an impenetrable facsimile of an agora, a simulacrum, a corporate center, "city of the corporations." How then do we develop politically efficacious speech, grounded in the fact of human numerousness, in a city whose images are all abstractions from elemental facts? The crisis in Oppen's poem—"How talk / Distantly of 'The People'"—is precipitated by anecdote, by his recollection of being *among the many* during his army service. When words cannot contain or recover or heal over the relation of individual experience to that place called the "crowd," poetry becomes feckless and surrenders to abstraction. Abstraction is the worst kind of existential divisiveness because it sets up as a desirable mental object an antihuman idea of the human separate from actual biological and social necessity. We've lived through this recently during the war in the Persian Gulf, with our arsenal of computer lights, pulsing beeps, and smart bombs, where death is imitated, mocked, by transitory perceptual stimuli. If, as Engels said, freedom is the recognition of necessity, then abstraction starves freedom. To Oppen the poet's task is to treat words as ghosts run wild in subways, the poet being a kind of spook-catcher chasing words underground in the hope that once caught they will bring meaning and sense. Aboveground, as the elemental regard of words rooted in necessity diminishes, public speech becomes more and more rootless; it becomes what Oppen calls "a ferocious mumbling."

A private task it is, but for public effect. And a tragic task in at least one respect. The American poet is familiar with a divisiveness that cannot be healed over. In section twenty of "Of Being Numerous" we're riding the subway in the 1960s. The passengers—the "they" that includes the poet regarding them—are waiting for war, more war, news of war, knowing the passion of that expectation and the passion of the destruction to come. The mood of the passage is tense, sick with the blend of exhilaration and dread. Then there is a turn: "They know / By now as I know / Failure and the guilt / Of failure." And Oppen remembers it is like the nervous anticipation in "Hardy's poem of Christmas," where we imagine and hope to find "in the sheds of a nation / Farm animals, / Draft animals, beasts for slaughter." Hardy's "The Oxen" is about the migratory imagination seeking refuge in familiar (though no longer tenable) images of devotional unity. For Oppen, if we were to find the animals there, it would mean they have forgiven us, "or which is the same thing, / That we do not altogether matter." The first degree of political tragedy is that the mind holds and the body feels as true that which both at once realize to be dream dust. The second and intenser degree is described in remarks made not long ago by Claude Lévi-Strauss. Asked to define myth, he said that an American Indian would say a myth tells of time before humans and animals became distinct beings. "No situation seems more tragic, more offensive to heart and mind, than that of humanity coexisting and sharing the joys of a planet with other living species yet being unable to communicate with them." Failing to recover that lost time, yet feeling in our deepest sense the desire for such unity, we would wish forgiveness from the other orders of life on earth even while we pulse with dread and thrill over more war. That's the terrifying compound a poet of political intelligence confronts and struggles to express.

"Of Being Numerous" ends with a prose bit cribbed from Whitman's letter to his mother, describing the Capitol and the Genius of Liberty figure recently mounted atop it. Oppen's work generally is a criticism of Whitman's headlong expansionist poetics. He sets off from the prose paragraph (dated 1864, after Whitman had served as a volunteer medic and had written about the heaps of amputated limbs around the hospital camp) its final word:

The sun when it is nearly down shines on the [Genius of Liberty's] headpiece and it dazzles and glistens like a

Public Music

41

big star: it looks quite
curious . . .

Oppen, who once said that Whitman's "deluge and soup of words is a screen for the uncertainty of his own identity," distributes the historicized material so that it conforms to his own halting, deliberative, probing idiom. He makes use of Whitman's own language to revise, rhythmically, his celebratory project. Oppen's own project is not vocative or expansionist. His language does not summon or shout. His words, as public offering, calibrate consciousness as it secretes its crucial sentences about love, perception, and destiny. In a note on Thomas McGrath and other Old Left poets, he wrote, "It can be observed . . . that when we say 'moral' we mean that which concerns the destiny of humanity." His own intention was to make poems that had moral purpose and therefore, as he says elsewhere, would express a concept of humanity, "something we want humanity to be or to become, [which] would establish the basis of an ethic."

Poets have an austere sense of being singular subjects (Oppen's "the singular / Which is the bright light of shipwreck") confronting the indiscriminate feelings of a crowd. A useful poetic language, however much evolved from tradition, is essentially an idiolect, and that sets poets apart from the crowd for whom or toward whom they write. Modern poets have had to live maybe more self-consciously than their predecessors with the fact of linguistic estrangement as a necessary condition for making statements that will be directed ultimately at the communal good, statements that are exemplary attempts at moral discrimination. This estrangement may be what Yeats had in mind when he said that poets are good citizens turned inside out. In the public sphere, politicians have not so much co-opted a common language as they have shown with grotesque verve that any speech purporting to be common idiom, as a voice of the people, is Geryon's speech. This, too, is a poet's proper subject, the imposture and fraudulent sincerity of public speech.

In fact, the complete political poet is probably one who dares to allow into poetry Geryon's smoothie voice or soapbox sincerities or delusional outcries as necessary poisons immunizing poetry against the falsehood of self-interested speech.

Anything a poet writes measures some estrangement between the poet and the polis. For the true idiolect, moreover, there can be no correct or acceptable point of view. During the antihierarchical rage of the counterculture in the late 1960s, whose efforts as a mass against the Vietnam War he entirely supported, Oppen knew that the death of singular art in favor of "art for the people" meant the death of individual meditative dissent and therefore the weakening of political intelligence in society at large. Poets cannot finesse idiosyncrasy so that it seems populist or communal. (Or if they can, it's tribute paid to Geryon.) All one can do, finally, is to eat the contradiction and make it part of one's materials. Better that than improvised solidarity or heat-seeking sloganeering. For Oppen the political lay in writing truthfully one's perceptions, not arguing one's beliefs. Bad poetry, he said, is poetry "tied to a moral or a political (same thing) judgment."

And yet the most idiosyncratic verse, if it is political, has something in it that aspires to choral crowd music. I sometimes think the intense personalism of American poetry in recent decades, with its psychological fussiness and maniacally modest self-absorption, is one sign of the failure of belief in the possibility of poetry as truly public music. In a 1969 letter Oppen says that before putting words down he thinks of his daughter, already twenty-seven years old, and knows she will read what he writes. This engages the scrupulous sense of a future, of the truth of a record kept and passed on. In those days he felt that the only real safety for him or her or any of us was to put the poems "in the public record . . . . And in the public music." Poetry thus adds to the store of moral deliberation, to specific imaginative concern for the destiny of humanity. Although his method of composition owed much to the precisionist example of Pound, Oppen said that the masculine energy of Pound's work and personality appalled him. In the poems he wrote after those twenty-five years of silence, Oppen went round and round the question of being numerous, "of being part of a human unity, a human entity." Sometimes his moral authority is a little oppressive (he is much esteemed as a "moral presence," but within famous moral presences lurk moral police) and it's mostly humorless. But the question of poetry's agency in the world is a real one. Oppen insisted that the poet's work is to see the one thing, not the thousand things. I would add that to see the one thing in consciousness of the world is always to see *in relation*— to the polity, to the Things, to the annals of anecdote, to poetry's formal past. And it's a happy task to intensify poetry's response to relatedness, not out of a dreary sense of poetical obligation, but rather out of fevered uncertainty and anxiety about its efficacy. I often think the first image of the poetic imagination is one of its own disappearance—words written on a fogged window, words lost in a passing car. Out of that original separation comes the need to put words in whole arrangements that have meaning and that express meaning.

The Tactics and Strategy of Thomas McGrath

For a poet like Thomas McGrath, concerned all his life with the political order and the patterns of authority that determine power relations (and therefore human suffering and solace), Ezra Pound would seem to be a useful, exemplary predecessor. The *Cantos* is an encyclopedic delirium of kinds and forms of authority—poetic, pedagogic, political, social, intellectual, and cultural. But to McGrath, revolutionary and one-time member of the Communist Party who in later years described himself as "unaffiliated far left," Pound was a pre-industrial, pre-nineteenth century sensibility hostage to the values of earlier ruling classes, to structures of hierarchy and the ordering willfulness of authority. McGrath's political formations were anarco-syndicalist. Born in 1916, he received his early political education on his father's North Dakota farm, where he worked the harvests and was surrounded much of the time by the Wobblies, Communists, and assorted radicals who were always welcome at the McGrath household. From their out-loud dreaming of revolution and new world order, and their stories of goon squads, scabs, and saboteurs, the young McGrath took an education at once theoretical and practical. In one episode of his long poem *Letter to an Imaginary Friend*, he tells how as a young boy he and his older brother Jimmy waited in ambush to assassinate a local banker who was evicting the McGrath's from their land. By the time he began to write *Letter* in 1955, he had formulated a distinction between what he called tactical and strategic poetry. Tactical poetry directs the will of its readers to action; it has immediate practical ends, is frequently keyed to events like a strike or factory fire, and assumes political sympathy on the part of its readers. Methodist hymns, "Onward Christian Soldiers," and Brecht's "The United Front Song" are poems of the type, as are some of the verses McGrath himself produced in his 1949 pamphlet, *Longshot O'Leary's Garland of Practical Poesie.* McGrath's tactical poems, though, were not welcomed by Old Left journals because of their ambiguities, cross-eyed humor, and tonal eccentricities. Strategic poetry is that which seeks not to stir or direct the will but to expand consciousness. (McGrath winced a little whenever he used that phrase, but he knew it was the accurate one.) Strategic poetry "arouses a feeling related to that expansion of consciousness," and his favorite example of the type was Neruda's *Canto Generale.*

Compound the two types and you have a poetry in which tactical immediacy supports and advances strategic purpose, in which the factual punch of dramatic event blends into the subversive, expansive manipulations of visionary poetry, and thus clarity and craziness, "absolute lucidity and purest, most marvelous bullshit." This is the ambition of *Letter to an Imaginary Friend,* where immediacy is supplied by remembered event and expanded consciousness is defined by McGrath's frequent assertion that Dakota is everywhere—Dakota, real legendary zone where "Tom McGrath's" political identity was forged. He declares the ambition in the opening of part two:

And I am only a device of memory
To call forth into this Present the flowering dead and the living
To enter the labyrinth and blaze the trail for the enduring journey
Toward the rounddance and the commune of light.

Letter is driven by memory's authority to realize the world's time in the poem's present: "All time condenses here. Dakota is everywhere. The world / Is always outside this window." Its strategic mission is to prophesy a time when a new relation between humans and the things of the world will exist. As recently as 1976 McGrath was saying: "We must try to find our real relationship to things." *Letter* is also driven by changefulness, process, violent undoings, and vehement assertions of what has been left undone, and it agonizes over the familiar incoherencies of actuality and vision. In the *Cantos*, Pound argued that political and cultural renewal and wholeness began in chaos and incoherence: "Wilderness of renewals, confusion / Basis of renewals, subsistence, / Glazed green of the jungle." McGrath meets Pound in his own rhetorical intent: "Out of imperfect confusion to argue a purer chaos."

McGrath said his poem is political in that "it hopes to invent and restructure the past and the future by using the narrative line of the speaker of the poem and events from personal and political-social history to create the 'legend' of these times." He will tell legend before fact because it stills reality into scenes that represent a culturally specific but representative past and a humanely general future. His loyalty to political purpose is exercised as loyalty to the poem, to the emergence of language from the stir of image life in the mind and heart, with visionary inquisitiveness as the determining element. But the imagination, I believe, is essentially instinctive, spendthrift, and prodigal. It is not by nature conservative. Erudition, ordinary recollection, fact-hounding, the plying of evolved forms—these are poetry's conservative activities. Happy natural antagonists, the prodigal and the pedant tease out all sorts of unforeseen dilemmas in the course of writing. Though McGrath is more of an ideologue than Pound, his poem is flattest and most inconsequential when it's doing its most extravagant strategic work. *Letter* sags not when McGrath directs the will toward political change but rather when the language too promiscuously generates its own inventions. McGrath's protagonist is a vagrant pupil of revolution, and the dramatic work required to move him from episode to episode, and to prophesy the developing vision of a changed world, brings about a hyperactive sameness, a hallucinatory blur, colorful and rapid, but indistinct. The poem cannot outsmart itself. For the poet to say that his poem "is merely what happens / now / On this page," may affirm its legendary quality, but it also alerts us to the fact that the poem is a sequence of instances, rushes, prophetic improvisations; it does not guarantee that what happens will be progressive or even different from one page to the next.

One charge of the political poet is to bear memory like hard freight. Memory is the burden of history suffered, of experience viewed always as a particular situated in a crowd, the single body or soul in the magnetic field of common suffering. McGrath calls his poem "pseudo-autobiography," which I take to be a dispensation of the imagination's prodigal wrath and ruckus, a dispensation to situate particular acts of witness in the more comprehensive activity of dreaming on behalf of the tribe. *Letter* is a tablet of names of those who suffered humiliation, exile, and death: Cal and Mac (young McGrath's models for anarchic self-offering) and Jimmy McGrath (the older brother and would-be co-assassin who died in World War II) are the dominant figures. They are not only dramatic presences in the poem but are also historical flares throwing general light on a scene. One decisive scene occurs early on, during a harvest strike organized by Cal, a drifter who acts as young McGrath's hero and mentor. The strike is broken by McGrath's uncle who, enraged by what he sees as petulant unproductive activism, punches out Cal and gets the men back to work. It's a moment of absolute, unhealable rupture of affections and allegiances: between family clan and workers' family; blood relative and ideological brother; family authority and true teacher; boss and fellow worker. The task for McGrath or any poet who would ground prophecy in idiosyncratic events is to hold simultaneously a revolutionary hypothesis, in all its abstract inhuman clarity of design and purpose, along with the actual situation-specific suffering of time's chancy flux. The poem's busted grandeur is built in nearly equal measures of dramatic intelligence and repetitive prophetic assertiveness, and the poem's greatest defect is its failure to realize both at once.

One of McGrath's intellectual heroes was Christopher Caudwell, the pseudonym of Christopher St. John Sprigg, a prolific journalist, pulp novelist, poet, and Marxist critic who died at the age of thirty fighting in the International Brigade in Madrid. Caudwell believed in the power of poetry to redefine our relation to things and thereby alter consciousness. His theoretical task was to absorb into his model of a politically responsive and socially responsible poetry the traditional dream-visioning subjectivity of the imagination, to fuse a vision of the common dance with the eccentric particulars of individual existence. This is the task McGrath tries to execute in his poem. His method is to make language serve as heroic legend of individual suffering and mass atrocity. Language, in any poetry, has to live against the heavy odds of selective forgetfulness that the mind exacts, making liars of us when we most zealously claim to have arrived at inclusive, indisputable truth. The lists we encounter in McGrath's poem are often a revolutionist's ledger and a restorative litany of things not to be forgotten: "Heavy the weight / of Jim, of Jack, of my father, of Cal, of Lambrakis, Grimau, / Hiroshima, Cuba, Jackson." As another strategy to fuse the common with the idiosyncratic, McGrath opens his poem to the sublime florid melancholy of Spanish surrealism; the fervent Lorca-inspired metaphors make all reality an animated relation:

> Terror of the time clock mechanical salaams low pressure systems
> Blowing out of the nightbound heart's high Saharas,
> A muezzin of blood blazing in a cage built out of doves.

Voices call to him in sleep, announcing the mission: "Hey there, resurrection man! ghost haunter, crazy damn poet." Damned poet, too, for he walks so much among shades, questioning them, his mentors, those who bore witness before him. The poem is, classically, his deposition. But because he is political, he has to resist the call to find luxuriant solace in the rolls of the dead. To dream away remembrance in that kind of lotus bed would be "to offer my body to the loud crows and the crass / Lewd jackals of time and money, the academy of dream-scalpers." To Auden's fatigued maxim that poetry makes nothing happen, McGrath offers his own wooly assertion that the poet is charged with

The Tactics and Strategy of Thomas McGrath

altering the world. To expand consciousness, to exemplify how the heart goes about finding a real relationship to things, is to make something happen. McGrath's intent, practicing "armed revolutionary memory," is to usher change by putting the very process of writing poetry in the contested zone between the materially resolved, complacent present and an inchoate revolutionary future, which for him means a classless society with equitably distributed wealth and work available for all, work that is expression and extension of the nature of the human. The exhibitionist prodigies of the poem's language serve this end. In the childhood confession scene in part three, the boy McGrath, in search of noteworthy sins, recites a litany of words whose mysterious presences have loomed from the pages of his reading. He confesses to minerology, barratry, chrestomathy, and catechresis. The delirium of the scene (the priest chimes in, trumping the boy's extravagance) tangles us in the real subject, the use of language as clerical tool, as an I.D. card to closed societies, as hierarchy built on shared or enforced ignorance.

Another revolutionary intent of *Letter* is to "angelize" pagan entities, to beatify what traditional Judeo-Christian hierarchies have demonized. McGrath's first step in doing this is to insist that the human and natural orders make up an interrelated whole, that the human is one element in the interfused, interdependent activity of material reality. Human kind does not, in McGrath's scheme, possess either material or spiritual lordship over the things of the world, and nature does not exist to serve the expropriative prerogatives of human need. This vision of restored holistic relations is not new, though its Marxist apparatus and its often abrasive and violent dramatization set it well apart from more pacific versions. Modern industrial society, in McGrath's view, can be revolutionized only by a new mind, one that will allow material relations to be modeled on a spiritual commonality that he calls the Round Dance. (A revolutionary situation exists, therefore, when material circumstances are about to dissolve into a chaos out of which may emerge new social formations grounded in a redefined spiritual nature.) The two

The Tactics and Strategy of Thomas McGrath

metaphors McGrath uses to sustain his Blakean inversion of heaven and hell, however, make me think that as his poem got longer he became too caught up in its systemic delirium. (After finishing parts one and two in 1968, McGrath thought he was finished, only to find that he had more to say; parts three and four were completed in 1984.) In part three he brings in elements from medieval kabbalistic cosmologies. He chants the names of his angelized demons: "Cham, Amoymon, Marx, Engels, Lenin, Azael, / Stalin, Mahazael, Mao, Sitrael—Che-Kachina." The list, equitably ranking side by side occult demiurges, authors of police states, political theorists, and the director of genocide against his own people, is more outrageous than any of Blake's terms in his marriage of heaven and hell, but it is historically vile and indiscriminate. What concerns me here, though, is that last entry, which announces a metaphor that runs more aggressively and purposefully than any other in the poem.

Hopi materials appear significantly in part two of *Letter to an Imaginary Friend*, and they dominate the poem's prophetic finale in part four. Material from Native American culture comes naturally to McGrath. We learn in the poem that as a boy his father took refuge for a week in Fort Ransom during an Indian scare, and the poet says somewhere that the Indian is the first wound in American consciousness. But McGrath's local culture is high plains, not southwestern. Why Hopi material? Why kachina? Frank Waters rhapsodically describes kachina as "the invisible forces of life manifesting themselves through the spirits of the clouds, lightning, color-directions, the heroes, the dead; through the masks representing them; and through the men who impersonate them; the breath of life which equally permeates rocks, trees, grass, all animals, men." I think McGrath takes over this material because the Hopi not only possess arguably the most coherent and articulated vision of religious-political existence, but they still maintain and practice this vision as a tribal-village unit. McGrath takes over a good deal from their culture. He applies kachina not only to Che Guevara but also to his own poem, kachina as companion, guide, prayer-celebrant, safe conduct to a new mind and new world. He brings into the poem the Hopi belief that their current lives are spent in the Fourth World, *Tuwaqachi*, an imperfect place where they are prey to trouble, bad thoughts, dissension, and divisiveness. But this will be followed by a better place, a Fifth World, *Saquasohuh*, whose coming will be heralded by a sign, the Blue Star Kachina. The Blue Star's assistance in the creation of *Saquasohuh* McGrath considers to be "a revolutionary act to create a revolutionary society."

I found these passages irritating when I first read them, because it seemed that McGrath, enemy of expropriators, was indulging in arbitrary cultural colonizing, appropriating a vision of sacred meaning as a prop in a secular political vision. Poets of course take over those metaphors that in the end most powerfully complete their vision. And violation or sacrilege may be necessary to make a new, more comprehensive, more intensely spiritual order. I think now this must have been McGrath's purpose, though I still reject his opportunistic use of Hopi material, especially in the facile, sound-linked association of Che and kachina and in the willed, celebratory invocations of the Blue Star that occur more frequently as the poem draws to an end. I think McGrath knew he was into some trouble. He declares himself an atheist, has fun with the story of Christ ("Jerusalem Slim"), yet makes a theistic system the core metaphor in his poem. He asserts that the poem's project is "To make sacred what was profane." He wants myths without gods, which perhaps identifies him as a political intelligence formed in the 1940s. He is a nonbeliever who, in his vision of existence, understands as Pound did that a just political order requires spiritual vitality and relatedness. But idiosyncratic desire causes him to rip kachina from its ceremonial, liturgical matrix. He needs kachina to be of use, but its use in *Letter to an Imaginary Friend* drains its energy, in part because it is used so selectively—kachina is a healer and a terrifier, essential but also theatrical, and it requires masks—and because it is made to *serve* the political will.

McGrath felt more at home among the diffused, periodic energies of pagan presences than those of his Roman Catholic upbringing. He rejects the hierarchies of Christian cosmology and sees them as complicit in the view of nature as exploitable matter subservient to human kind. During the sled ride to Christmas Mass recalled in luxurious detail in part three, he sees "the abstract light of the Father's Heavenly Power" as that which "Put out the eyes of the stars and drained the life from the moon." Like Blake, McGrath rejects the abstractions of the Christian order for what he feels to be a more sensuous spiritual immediacy. The moon's glare is a "deathshine . . . / (All that the priests have left / Of the warm and radiant Goddess who once held all our hands.)." Those priests stand for any intermediary authority—scientist, teacher, poet, banker—that would estrange us from what we naturally are and abstract us from the streaming things of the world. The poem becomes more saturated with a sense of sacred oneness as it progresses, as McGrath writes more exclusively of his early years. His description of a childhood Christmas stands as an image of the Round Dance to come, and it's an image of love. McGrath has his ledger of affects: "And anger sustains me—it is better than hope—/ it is *not* better than / Love." *Letter* is a chiliastic script in rough draft, and its vision of political unity is authorized finally not by ideological orthodoxy but by a spiritual consistency, however vaguely articulated. The poet, talking like crazy among the shades, charged with infusing into the present some version of a revolutionary future, is the Hermetic wayfarer, the go-between, and is not above a little thievery. In the poem's final section, McGrath remembers carrying around a pomegranate wafer, baked by his grandmother and called a "Persephone." That's the poet's ticket to the Underworld; it weighs him down and sustains him there. (This reminds me of Pound's Canto 79: "'Eat of it not in the under world' / See that the sun or the moon bless thy eating / kore, kore, for the six seeds of an error.") The goddess cookie, springtime sweet baked in winter, is a memory chip, McGrath's safe conduct between the worlds of the living and the dead.

The Tactics and Strategy of Thomas McGrath

A Note on Hayden Carruth
and Personality

During his long career as a poet, critic, and editor, Hayden Carruth has spent a good deal of energy articulating his positions on certain issues. His views, worked out in his critical prose and expressed as part of the life of feeling in his poetry, are not polemical reflexes but provisional understandings kneaded into the activity of writing. I cannot think of another poet of his generation, except perhaps Adrienne Rich, whose meditations have covered so many essential moral concerns of poetry and life. What I want to address here is the question of personality, Carruth's remarks about personality, and how his views have influenced my own.

The summative statement occurs in section thirty of "The Sleeping Beauty," Carruth's book-length meditation on love, form, and poetry, published in 1982 then reissued in 1990 (by Copper Canyon Press) in a revised edition. Speaking of his beloved Rose Marie Dorn, who is the center of his meditations, but also of himself and of the process by which poems come into being, Carruth writes of what he calls "the completed person in personality" that rises slowly upward through the dark toward some defining or definitive light:

> Out from the bondage of blood and nerves,
> Beyond history, between the stars,
> Pure subjectivity in its spirit, its spiritual
> Outreaching and inreaching,
> For which no ceremony of love, no ritual,

No convention and no teaching
Can suffice, but only love transcendent in the wreck
Of the determinant world, love continually searching
Beyond love,
    the poem crawling upward through the dark.

This is the flowering of an idea that Carruth had been working out, so far as I can tell, in the ten year period between his 1967 review of Lowell's *Near the Ocean* and a later essay that appeared in *Sewanee Review* called "The Act of Love: Poetry and Personality." He uses the term "personality" more or less as it was used by Nicolai Berdyaev, though without Berdyaev's Christian application, to mean whole individual subjectivity, spirit and body and soul as a bundled indivisibility of being. Personality, in Carruth's words, "is a phenomenon of pure existence and occurs in what have been called existential moments," instants outside time, untouched by the determinations of history, biology, society. Human freedom, in this scheme, is the freedom of subjectivity struggling to express its presence as archetype. This assertion, made nearly twenty years ago, strikes against the grain of much of the criticism taught and practised these days in universities, where poems are believed to be reducible to their ideological or social determinants, and that existential moments are just one more intellectual fiction contrived by the dominant or "hegemonic" ideology. In the 1976 *Sewanee Review* essay, Carruth lamented what he saw to be a failure of authenticity, a miscarriage of personality in some of the poetry then being published and praised. Personality, he felt, was being practiced as solipsism: "Instead of responsibility to life, instead of responsibility to his own personality as archetype of life, the poet is now responsible to his own personality and nothing more." The abridgment of the existentialist ethic Carruth found in Berdyaev (an abridgment caused in part by careerist myopia) had led a fairly large part of our poetic culture to a "license to indulge the self."

I read Carruth's essay a few years after it appeared. By that time I had

A Note on Hayden Carruth and Personality

formed my own opinions about personality and its place in our poetry, partly in reaction to the kind of work that commanded so much attention in the mid- and late 1970s, the "postconfessional lyric" most of all, but mostly to find my way beyond the definitions and confinements of mere personal identity. I felt that personality as existentialist process had been trivialized in our poetry and reduced to a static, inauthentic contrivance. It seemed to me that personality had become a kind of cult object and that it enfeebled poetry's capacity to gather up the public world. (My feelings then seem to me now blustery and stuffy, but they burned in me because at issue was everything I considered essential to lyric poetry.) The cult of personality had displaced simple, inquisitive moral awareness. Casual preciosities of perception were valued over clear recognitions. Maybe this is still a salient quality of our poetry, maybe it is always salient in approved middlebrow styles. The escape from the coy intimacies of the postconfessional lyric into the more ample and inclusive registers of the discursive style proposed by Robert Pinsky in the late 1970s was also inadequate because it brought with it too much suburban fussiness and self-admiration.

At any rate, I was most of all wary of any coquettish, self-protective objectification of personality. To clarify these things to myself, as a means of writing my way from one day to the next, over against personality I set the little idol of experience, the encounter with all that is not the subject, not the *me*. While I believed that intensest subjectivity was the essence of lyric poetry, I wanted a subjectivity so fused to experience that the two could not be told apart, that somehow subjectivity could disintegrate in that amalgam. It was, I now see, a puritanical view, and at the time I was in fact very much under the sway of Perry Miller's extraordinary book on Jonathan Edwards. I failed to see that my position was too defensive and reactive, and that setting off personality against experience was an intellectual convenience which finally calcified both and took them too much out of the turbulent changefulness of life.

A Note on Hayden Carruth and Personality

I took instruction from Carruth's remarks. His crucial term is transcendence. He says in his essay that personality is a dynamic process that extends beyond the self, transcending it. This pulled me out of my own conception of personality as something static, a configuration, the willed exaltation of idiosyncrasy. He situates the issue in its proper place, in our world of constantly mixed and revised orders. He admits to some perplexity about the end or destination, what he calls the "toward-which," of transcendence, though late in the essay he speculates that the direction of that movement of the soul "is for each consciousness in its own personality to answer, and the answer will be in its own terms." Subjectivity, personality, is essentially action, or existentialist process, and it is the action of seeking something away from or other than its own articulated self. Poetry, in these terms, does not need to be an escape from personality. The escape that matters is the escape from the crass or mercantile or narrowly careerist solipsism that personality may lead to. Personality is not a condition, it is a way or passage. Moreover, Carruth believes it is a passage of inwardness. If personality and the urge for transcendence direct us *away*, they direct us *away toward* the interior, the mysterious center: "Transcendence is a pushing through the petals of memory and feeling toward the deeper center of the flower." Or, in the terms of the passage from *The Sleeping Beauty* that I started with, it is the process of crawling upward through the dark.

Carruth's poetry has been mostly the story of his own seeking. His work has acted as a self-interrogating moral instrument, though that is my term and he may cringe to hear it said of him, so wary is he of pieties and Arnoldian gravities. He says in his essay that the crucial act in the process of seeking is love, "spiritual love, the state of being of a pure existence, and the aesthetic emotion is the experience of that state." I find the purest expression of this in "This Song," a poem in *From Snow and Rock, From Chaos*. It gathers up observations during a walk in the fields of northern Vermont in early fall and makes that gathering an articulation of the journey of subjectivity—one stage of it, at least—and of personality seeking transcendence through love. He pictures himself walking not only in a time of day one September afternoon, but also in a spirit time, in "an old dissension / bright with fear." He takes notice, with an exact countryman's eye, of the vivid variety of field flowers, but he also sees how ferns "taken by frost, / made russet the fields and turned / the waysides yellow and brown."

His spirit life bleeds into the fall tones of the landscape. He realizes that he has wandered nearly all his life in this way, and that the object of the long search is "the touch that heals" and the "look that says *I know*." But there is no touch and no such look. The long Vermont winter is coming, and at its threshold—one of the many that have been and are to come—he still seeks what he knows does not wait for him. The last stanza tells what he finds:

> I feel September's little knives, and with my eyes
> I see bright spattered leaves in the matted
> grass. I hear this song, if it be a song: these
> insistent little bright fearful hesitant
> murmurs from high in the old pine trees.

What is this transcendence? I believe it is the pain and desire of the way of subjectivity described in his essay. In Carruth's terms, "This Song" is a love song. It's the cry of eros to find something other, once lost, that it may join and be healed, made finally sane and whole.

On Edwin Muir

Reviewing the *Collected Poems* in 1955, Edwin Muir criticized Wallace Stevens for following too obediently the aesthetic patterns contrived by his own mind, and for allowing his speculative nature to turn him away from life "to an imaginary world of beautiful objects, of peaches and pears." Stevens's desired world, even if occupied with things that satisfy the senses, remains a place which Muir calls "a legendary world without a legend." What he means, I think, is that Stevens's imagination, though much at ease among the fabulous, lacked the grounding and precedence of fable, that he could speculate on techniques of the mythy mind but did not possess such a mind. Frost was the more appealing poet, because he wrote about human action and choice as if they were already legend; Muir even singled out, in a 1943 review of Frost's work, the buck that crashes into view at the end of "The Most of It" as "a fine legendary image." Muir's critical judgments, like most of his poems, were rooted in his early experience. He was born and raised in the islands of Orkney, and in his *Autobiography* he writes about the ordinary blend of the fabulous and the normal in his native place: islanders sometimes encountered "fairicks" dancing on the shore in moonlight; a man who sailed out to find a mermaid returned to tell of his conversation with her; feats of great strength were reported and remembered as among the Achaeans; Muir's own father told him of witches that he knew. These were a few of the facts absorbed by the young boy who would later speak of childhood as the only period in life when we live in immortality because we are without a sense of the policing exactions of time. He describes childhood as a perfect unselfconscious repetition, "one day endlessly rising and falling." The ordinary activities of farm life fused in his young imagination to the heroic stories he heard from islanders and those he read in the few books available to him. When cows were brought to the bull he and the other children were shut inside the house, but to him the voices he heard in the yard were the cries of warriors fighting or playing heroic games. His poetry was a remaking or recapitulation of essential fables. His early life gave him not only subject matter but also legendary patterns on which he modeled narrative forms. In one of his late essays he remarked that "we become human by repetition." And poetry becomes more humane and more responsive to the whole of our existence by virtue of its recapitulations: "In the imagination that repetition becomes an object of delighted contemplation, with all that is good and evil in it, so that we can almost understand the saying that Hector died and Troy fell that they might turn into song."

Muir's people were tenant farmers subject to their landlords' needs. When Muir was fourteen his family had already worked three farms; the last of them was the worst, with dreary damp quarters and miserable land. That was when they decided to emigrate to Glasgow. Later he would recall life in Orkney as "a good order." That order, already destabilized by the tough existence on their last farm, was shattered when they moved to the city. Within two years his parents and two brothers were dead. The city did not destroy the family, though the circumstances of urban life did wear away the health of Muir's father. But the removal, the dislocation, took the family out of the familiar religious and social formations which sustained and to some degree protected them physically and spiritually. Muir soon commenced a succession of menial office jobs that allowed him to make his way in the world. One was in a bone factory in Fairport where for two years he breathed the stench of furnaces that reduced to charcoal carloads of maggot-covered bones. Orkney may have been a hardscrabble place, but there at least the elements of life, fabulous and actual, were fused into sensible rhythms, and the ancient order of guilt and sacrifice attached to the

On Edwin Muir

slaughtering of animals was still intact. Working in a bone factory, Muir was living through one kind of fall from a known, felt unity.

The story of the fall is often retold in his poetry, along with the dream of ritual purification and the restoration of a whole order. His adult intellectual life, in fact, can be mapped as a series of attempted restorations or, as I think of them, conversions, where the soul seeks to heal lesions, to mend its divisiveness. The *Autobiography* concludes with this:

> I was lucky to spend my first fourteen years in Orkney; I was unlucky to live afterwards in Glasgow as a Displaced Person. . . . Because a perambulating revivalist preacher came to Kirkwall when I was a boy, I underwent an equivocal religious conversion there; because I read Blatchford in Glasgow, I repeated the experience in another form, and found myself a Socialist. In my late twenties I came, by chance, under the influence of Nietzsche . . . . In my middle thirties I became aware of immortality, and realized that it gave me a truer knowledge of myself and my neighbors. Years later . . . I discovered that I had been a Christian without knowing it.

The becalmed, processional summation of his experience has the measured quality of much of his poetry—it's the plainness and orderly simplicity of fable.

By the time he began to write poetry at the age of thirty-five, after having launched himself as a critic and essayist, Muir was by his own report too old to be vulnerable to contemporary influences. He came to poetry an already formed intellectual, and he admitted that his deference toward ideas made his beginnings as a poet quite difficult. That deference never left him, and a distinguishing feature of his poems is that they are concept heavy. He could never quite express in poetry what it *feels* like to work a thought, and the mixed feeling-tones we often experience in moments of consciousness are so muted or thinned out in his poetry that they hardly seem to exist. His image world is more a bearer of ideas than of feelings. He felt that the task of the poet is "to make his imaginative world clear to himself . . . [but that] world in becoming clear may grow hard and shallow and obscure the mystery which it once embodied." Muir wanted to write a poetry that embodied the essential mysteries of existence and civilization. The danger of shallowness becomes all the greater when a poet's imaginative world exists, like Muir's, as a succession of emblematic settings, events, and personages stilled and heraldic like a frieze. He kept his world clear not by enlarging or diversifying his image hoard but by refining its essential concepts and by varying the fabulous contexts poem to poem. He is like the bard who tells the same story three ways, each time with a different shape and import but always recognizably the same.

In the *Autobiography* he writes that "there are times in every man's life when he seems to become for a little while a part of the fable, and to be recapitulating some legendary drama which, as it has recurred a countless number of times, is ageless." His poems are ritual enactments of this kind, and they do not concern themselves only with recapitulated human actions. Seasons exist for him as legends. In an early poem, "When the Trees Grow Bare On the High Hills," feeling the surprising buoyancy and weightlessness of things in autumn the poet becomes "Mere memory, mere fume / Of my own strife, my loud wave-crested clamor, / An echo caught / From the mid-sea / On a still mountain-side." The transformation of self into memory is some kind of purification ritual wherein finally "Attainment breathes itself out, / Perfect and cold." Muir seems to have believed the poet to be a permeable consciousness suffused at once by the instant and by the completed past—any poem then becomes a ritual offering of that consciousness, purified of personality. The haunted tone so peculiar to Muir's work comes from the way any moment in a poem can swim away in the echo chamber of the past's endless repetitions. His poems do not show the stress of deliberations, the kind of aggrieved scruples we hear in so much of Eliot's poetry; they present recapitulated suffering as if it were an unchanged moral sentence. In one of his finest poems, "Ballad of Hector in Hades," the Trojan hero is doomed to recall Achilles' pursuit and the chase around the walls of the city. (The poem recapitulates a childhood experience when Muir was chased home from school by a local bully.) Hector remembers, for himself and us, the bright beauty of the physical world, "The little flowers, the tiny mounds, / The grasses frail and fine." He remembers, too, how the bright world converges on his shame and all of nature bears witness to his flight: "The sky with all its clustered eyes / Grows still with watching me, / The flowers, the mounds, the flaunting weeds / Wheel slowly round to see." His own death is now legend in his consciousness, and the singular feeling tone is relief that his humiliation is over, though the image that concludes the poem is the one we know must repeat in Hector's mind: "While round bright Troy Achilles whirls / A corpse with streaming hair."

The fall of Troy is one of the recurrent legends in Muir's poetry. Its destruction and the dispersal of its inhabitants represented for him the wartime devastations and displaced populations of the 1930s and 1940s. Legends survive in large part because they are essentially static, unchanging, always somewhat aloof from the rattlings and travails of daily life. They lie beyond fact. Muir's enterprise was to disclose the legendary within familiar facts. In "Troy" an old man "so venerable / He might have been Priam's self, but Priam was dead," lives among Troy's sewers, fighting off the rats that have overtaken the city. Looters capture, torture, and interrogate him, "Asking: 'Where is the treasure?' till he died." In another poem, "A Trojan Slave," we see the idea-trace even more darkly drawn. Thirty years after the fall of his city, the old slave regards his master as "a Grecian dolt, / Pragmatic, race-proud as a pampered colt." For all his hatred of the Greeks, a "cold aspiring race," his deeper spite is reserved for the Trojans who, even as their city fell, refused to arm their servants: "And while they feared the Greeks they feared us most." The war, as the slave reviews it, was a system of fatal vanities built up on class and racial arrogance. The disintegration of class distinctions and racial divisiveness was one of the aspirations of the Socialism that Muir embraced in his early twenties (though he detested the Marxist view of necessary class war), and we hear it in the slave's view of what could have saved Troy. But there is also in the slave's monologue the sourness and anger of Nietzschean *ressentiment*, that source of power and righteousness for the disenfranchised which, Nietzsche argued, was at the center of the rise of Judeo-Christian morality. For the slave, the fall of the great city remains, "as if in spite, a happy memory."

Muir's 1924 collection of essays *Latitudes* contains a piece titled "A Note on the Scottish Ballads" in which he says that Scottish writers usually come from humble ranks whereas English writers most often come from the cultivated classes. Though he had no university education, Muir became an extremely cultivated man, a much sought after translator and reviewer, but these structures were built on the bedrock of Orkney culture. The plainness of his poems—I mean not just the unadorned diction but also the preservation of event and figure as primeval foreground—speaks for an ambition he saw realized in the ballads: "The ballads go immediately to that point beyond which it is impossible to go, and touch the very bounds of passion and of life." But Muir was too much a pious ironist, and became too much a European intellectual, to touch those extremities in his work. His poems are filled with elemental settings and actions which do not of their own possess elemental feelings. Poems like "The Town Betrayed," "The Return of Odysseus," "The Interrogation," "Outside Eden," the beautiful "The Transfiguration" and many others are pageant presentations of life; they *present* the "passion, terror, instinct, action" that he found and cherished in ballad literature, but they don't seethe with the experience of those intensities. The textures of actuality have not been brought over into the language textures. This has something to do with the meditative

On Edwin Muir

quality of Muir's work. He praises ballads for their energy, their refusal of meditative delay, their "ecstatic living in passion at the moment of its expression and not on reflection, and the experiencing of it therefore purely, as unmixed joy, as complete terror." We sometimes most admire that which lies beyond our own temperamental capacities or which we feel is irrecoverable. Muir admired in the ballads that complete, oblivious inhabiting of momentary feeling, of elemental joy, fear, or sorrow, which his own poetry does not enact, cannot enact because it is so mediated by reflection. His poems powerfully illustrate, exemplify, and report sudden passion, they do not embody it. Scenic clarity and the high relief of anecdote matter more to him than emotional intensity, and his favorite imaginative arrangement is of figures in a landscape.

The series of poems he wrote in the early 1940s with titles like "The Threefold Place," "The Original Place," "The Unattained Place," and so forth, are mostly about imaginary homecomings and original places. Home, stranger, man and woman, "leaf and bird and leaf," threshold, city walls, messengers, "silver roads"—these are the figures and landmarks in the poems. They have the simplicity Muir valued in the ballads, but they are presented with a self-awareness not found there. "The Sufficient Place" is a legend about what suffices, the moment in consciousness when balance and peace obtain in a household while "All outside / From end to end of the world is tumult." The household, the man and woman standing at the threshold "simple and clear / As a child's first images," are set forth as mythic categories: "This is the Pattern, these the Archetypes." That intellectual theatricalization, the self-conscious designation of the vision, marks a reflective estrangement that the poems themselves time and again seek to overcome. In the most unsettling of this group, "The Dreamt-of Place," Muir dreams he sees two birds cutting across the air like Dante's two mating doves, Paolo and Francesca, leading the souls lost to love. But this is a place untroubled by orthodox judgment, free from damnation. The old god does not rule here: "The nightmare god was gone / Who roofed their pain." Hell greens out and becomes a natural continuation of *il dolce mondo* aboveground. The dead and the living reconcile into one continuity:

> This is the day after the Last Day,
> The lost world lies dreaming within its coils,
> Grass grows upon the surly sides of Hell,
> Time has caught time and holds it fast for ever.

First world, last world, dream world are all one in the poem, and they compose the kind of visionary tableau Muir was finest at creating. His clearest signature, however, comes with the turn in the last few lines. Within his dream-vision of the place of redemption, of unity and harmony, comes a thought: "Where is the knife, the butcher, / The victim? Are they all here in their places? / Hid in this harmony? But there was no answer." The mind and heart can put the question to the dream, but the dream—legendary, heraldic, typical—is unresponsive, sealed off, keeping its own mysterious wisdom. Muir's imagination never strayed far from Eden's gate, from the sedate perfections of the Golden Age, but this inclination was jolted and countered by the experience of his own disordered nightmarish time. What dream of a golden place can keep down bloodguilt, paranoia, and the knowledge of genocide? This poem is one of his finest because it tells with massiveness and credibility and completeness the simple story of a dream-persuasion overturned by waking doubt, waking knowledge. But that suspicion comes to us at such a vulnerable moment, when we have already been converted by the authority of the imagination of the dream, that we are then drawn even closer to some final derangement.

When he writes of refugee populations, outcasts of Paradise, homeland, town, or family (the images in Ingmar Bergman's *Shame* could have been modeled on Muir's poetry) he often inducts himself among "the always homeless, / Nationless and nameless." His "we" is an autobiographical fact; after leaving Orkney he spoke of himself as a Displaced

Person. It is also a moral and political commitment to suffer history among others, to negotiate moral qualities in a world where Nietzsche's project of the transvaluation of all values seemed to have gotten stuck terrifyingly halfway, half-realized, a monstrous intellectual creature whose handsome but unfinished leonine and raptor features were blended into beautiful but not fully articulated human ones. In "The Good Town," once all the normal balances of moral relation are disrupted by two wars and their ensuing occupations, all those clarities are made opaque by the new mediators—policemen, informants, collaborators. The change causes the teller of the tale, a townsman, to question what they all (perhaps too complacently) regarded as the essential goodness of their place and which now seems to have been "conquered" by evil. He realized, though, that moral balance is not governed like fluid levels: you cannot readjust it by increasing or decreasing quantities, or by controlling local pressures and gravities. The bad, in order to succeed, may take on the color of the prevailing good. The good, intact but enslaved, may take on the hue of the wicked in order to pass unnoticed, unpunished: "We have seen / Good men made evil wrangling with the evil, / Straight minds grown crooked fighting crooked minds." The poem, for all its cool archetypal presentation, describes actual historical patterns lived out by populations in occupied territories (and even more exactly by the experiences of partisan cadres throughout Europe in the 1940s). It all tells us how the failure of the will to question and refine the moral-political values we hold most dear, and most (pridefully) representative, will weaken those same values and induce a complacency that breeds corruption and equivocation. The populace described in "The Good Town" have become moral refugees; they live in their native place as displaced souls.

Muir somewhere says that Eden's gate is everywhere and nowhere. That also describes the center of a labyrinth, as well as the disorientation induced by night crossings, border flights, interrogations, displacements without destinations. In "The Labyrinth" Theseus, or Thesean consciousness, has finally escaped the maze, which was a condition of pure alienation, perfect of its kind with a center everywhere and all else undifferentiated "place." Once restored to "its enemy / The lovely world," Theseus suffers the maze in memory, in his ordinary experiences of "all the roads / That run through the noisy world, deceiving streets / That meet and part and meet, and rooms that open / Into each other." He has a dream vision that momentarily dissolves the labyrinth's after-image which so confuses his life, a vision of a world overseen by gods, "each sitting on top of his mountain-isle." The round of human events, the repetitions of birthdays, marriages, holidays, of "Ploughing and harvesting and life and death," exist within the harmonies made by the gods' conversation. Everything is woven into harmonious celestial dialogue. It's a vision of the Peaceable Kingdom as a perfect sentence. And that, now, is the real world to Theseus, though it exists only as one vision in the image-hoard that also includes the recurrent dream of the maze that concludes the poem. That repeated dream knocks the dreamer back into his alienated life; whenever it recurs he wakes to feel momentarily lost: "Oh these deceits are strong almost as life. / Last night I dreamt I was in the labyrinth, / And woke far on. I did not know the place."

Muir's entire career can be viewed as a struggle against what he described in a 1949 essay on Spengler as the cry of historical necessity over the life of the individual. He was converted to Socialism in his twenties, but he could not accept Marxism, which he felt makes the historical process "the sole significant embodiment of life." He believed that while humankind works out its destiny in time, in history, its meaning in the world and to itself derives from the soul's immortality. Muir knew that the artistic mind shares this view with the religious mind. The view has a pragmatic virtue in that "it gives meaning to the actual life we live, and accounts to us for ourselves." Out of this comes his concept of the imagination, stated late in life in *The Estate of Poetry*, as "that power by which we apprehend living beings and living creatures in their individuality, as they live and move, and not as ideas or categories." As a definition grounded in elemental sympathy, it is winning but too nice. Muir's poetics finally are circumscribed by a sense of decency, of human goodness and sympathy, which verges sometimes on advocacy and which in the rhythms and language of his verse is transmuted into sober, diligent, modest normalcy. While he removes the human from the mechanical press of history, he refits the individual into a legendary narrative which itself tends to be overdetermining. Muir is certainly a religious poet by his own definition, but he is one who in the language of his poems abjures sacred decoration; and although we hear tell of aspiration and grief and joy in his poetry, we are seldom brought close to the incoherent cravings and indecencies of appetite and need, or the shriek of want and sorrow. His ambition to pursue our originating fables in the ordinary experience of the modern individual, and to conduct the pursuit in an almost puritanically plain style, equipped him to retell what he called "the great and the little glooms."

Shooting the Works

Charm

You're walking on a beach and find a small stone, nearly round and worn smooth except for a prickly spur or notch, some flaw that breaks up the curvilinear perfection the friction of sea and sand has contrived. The irregularity, its oddness, its completed imperfectedness, gives it special value. If it were sweetly roundly beautiful, you might throw it back or take it home and add it to your collection, on a shelf, behind glass. Throw it away or display it—it makes no difference. But because of its flawed or disrupted form, you put it in your pocket and keep it there, an amulet, to bring good fortune or beat away bad, precisely because it does *not* fit right and good in the cavity of your fist.

Fifteen years ago, living in south Louisiana, I sometimes went to an informal gathering of poets from the area. It was the usual sort of get-together of people who were writing and wanted a neighborhood of criticism. (I was teaching composition at the local state university; I was the only one in our group who had not been in a writing workshop.) By that time I had written poems that would later be in a book called *The Only Dangerous Thing*, in which I tried to tell a pattern of emigration, a passion of dispersal and cultural dispossession that was part of my own history and seemed also a general American story. I brought a few of the poems to one of our meetings, and the only comment I still remember is that the poems lacked charm. I'd never heard that word used to describe a desirable quality of poetry—used by a writer, I mean—and it confused me. I knew charm to be poetry's first, Orphic power, when the music of voice and words falls upon the wild things of the world and stills them for the duration of the song. But this is charm as enchantment, a narcotic power that draws on the savage entanglements of magic and nature. My critic had something more social in mind, a quality of collegial amenity, the preservation of experience in forms that can be processed by readers or listeners without too much anxiety. I knew my work lacked the Alexandrian finesse that I enjoyed in the work of others. My critic seemed to be looking for a self-aware and self-gratifying pleasurability in the movement of words, in an image, in the conclusive reasoned sense made of an occasioning experience, a pleasurability unmistakably pitched in a way that would appeal to an audience. "These poems," he said, "have no charm."

He was right. I remembered that Catullus was a charmer, in his abrasive way, and that Raleigh and Spenser and Sidney were aulic charmers. But I wanted, then and now, something different. I write to satisfy myself, but I don't want the poems to wear the glamor of self-satisfaction or glow with the pleasures of their own perceptions. I am not much concerned with the social pitch of the poems, with a community's shared assumptions about what might be pleasurable. When I was in college, two of my models were Crane and Yeats, so from the beginning my notion of charm involved an unstable compound of sensuous energy and high finish—it meant pushing language nearly to collapse or incoherence. The only charm that mattered, and matters to me still, is of the kind borne by that sea stone. Charm as a barely containable power, good or bad medicine, fateful, attractive but not always pleasurably so. Its aura might allure readers, but not at the expense of jagged attention and acute regard; it does not seek their approval, only their love. Charm inheres not in genteel contrivances and satisfying resolutions and anecdotal coziness, but in the confusions of surprise, unevenness, disruption, and excess, in the nasty spur or notch on the polished surface. Charm as protection, too, the sweet garlic-braid cloud of stink warding off pieties, boilerplate niceties, "interesting observations," and honeyed sense.

Form

Not form. Rather, *formal values*, which takes in the sense of registers, relatedness, tonalities, precarious balances, detonated (and detonating) patterns, colorist extravagance distorting and breaking up the definitions of good drawing, Keats's "candied apple, quince, and plum, and gourd; / With jellies soother than the creamy curd, / And lucent syrops, tinct with cinnamon." Or *plastic values*, which takes in the sense of pliability, thingness, shape emergent from conflict, provisional conclusions and contested resolutions, the motions of language in patterns, motions that are themselves events of feeling. Formal values are not instrumental, for they do not give voice to an already scored concept or pattern. (A poet wants signature effects as irreducible and as "formalist" as Titian red, without surrendering or dissolving the use of language as value deliberator.) These values are primary and expressive and in a constant state of definition. They remain indefinite until struck, coined, in the form of a finished poem, fixed in the scheme of words. At least until the poet revises it. One of the severe, delicious pleasures of writing is that the definition of a poem is arrived at only through the provocations of uncertainty and indefiniteness, the restless and essentially discontented (happy discontent!) plying and proofing of syllable, idiom, and line that seeks to destabilize what has come perhaps too easily into a structure.

I realize that my sense of formal values can become a piety of its own. Just then, though, I mistyped "formal values" as "floral values." Decoration, but also knockout fragrance. Which goes to illustrate my point. Error, misprision, unsettledness and migratory instinct, the river Alph coursing through its measureless unlit caverns bearing pimply stones and other debris in its underworld passage before it emerges near the sunlit pleasure dome, and the deliberations by which these disordered and disordering powers are made over into coherent expressions of existence, *and* the scorelines and stains and coincidental bucklings of the process brought over into the actual finish of the work—these taken together make up my working sense of form. I take the formalizing impulse in poetry to mean the will and desire to destabilize what's given, and that the most conscientious loyalty to a tradition is expressed by pressuring those established patterns from the inside out. Folded into this, obviously, is an awareness of metrical practice. Metrical pattern and variation is no Platonic idea. It is one element in the constellation of formal values that stir in the phantasmagoria of consciousness. The poets who interest me most are often those who write in contested meters, where I can feel that metrical stability, as it has been historically defined and revised, is in a fairly constant state of being challenged or destabilized or brought into a fresher definition by its own contents of feeling. I find it in massive, condensed form in Bunting's *Briggflatts*, spread here and there throughout Williams (whose mysterious assertions about "measure" and "structure" I feel I understand a bit only when I'm writing, when they are being worked as part of the instinct for form), and in its most bullying expression in Lowell. Many poems by Thom Gunn and Alan Dugan sound at once exquisitely traditional and edgily, crankily of our moment, because of their rude, assertive handling of "tradition." If they charm, they do so at their own risk.

Most of those in recent years who have been called, or who call themselves, New Formalists are essentially illustrators. Form for them is instrumental, not substantive; it annotates or describes emotion but is not expressive of emotion. For these poets, form may be entirely articulated by the mere shape of anecdotal content. I never feel in their work any internal force pushing or pulling the language. It is an exceedingly polite poetry, its language mostly at ease in its own equilibrium and unperturbed knowingness. It takes the complex, painfully adjustive concepts of the Aristotelian mean and flexible ruler and turns them into a justification for handily-arrived-at moral sentences for the good life. This kind of poetry has its pleasures, and only a fool would deny them or their considerable power to charm. They are the pleasures of civilized decoration, an impeccable scrollwork casting its shadows on finely detailed wallpaper. But such poetry mistakes good manners for formal values. The kind of writing I prefer may not be any more desirable than decorative art, but it is surely something quite different. It is the difference between the poised, ungainsayable, self-absolving melancholy of Philip Larkin, and the inquisitive, volatile, punishing formal dynamics of W. S. Graham or Geoffrey Hill.

History

Mircea Eliade often spoke of the terror of history, "the feeling experienced by a man who is no longer religious, who therefore has no hope of finding any ultimate meaning in the drama of history, and who must undergo the crimes of history without grasping the meaning of them." Captive Israelites knew their suffering had meaning because it was Yahweh's mysterious will at work. Hegel found meaning in events because they were manifestations of Universal Spirit. But in our time, as Eliade saw it, events are so emptied of transhistorical significance that the course of history, the narrative we enact and scrutinize, is trapped in its own cell of self-reference. History thus becomes a terror to be endured for biological reasons only, for species survival. We live in the present, those of us who are not true believers, without any sense of transcendent moral sponsorship, and we experience a neurotic dread, a sense of deprivation and estrangement, and a panic, that were in some ways mitigated by religious belief in most civilizations that have preceded our own. When Salman Rushdie was condemned to death by the Ayatollah Khomeini for blasphemies against Islam in *The Satanic Verses*, the astonished outrage many Westerners felt made it clear that, quite apart from the viciousness of the decree, its absolutism and divine sanction insulted our secular sense of justice, fair play, and mercy. It was not, in fact, Islam that condemned Rushdie but its theocrat the Ayatollah, acting at least as much for political reasons, to unite his subject nation. But insofar as orthodox Islam does not live in the terror of history, the Ayatollah's actions, vicious as they were, were coherent. To Westerners, however, Rushdie's condemnation was, in Eliade's terms, one element in the "blind play of economic, social, or political forces, or, even worse, only the result of the 'liberties' that a minority takes and exercises on the stages of universal history."

Even for those who feel themselves an active part of the Judeo-Christian tradition, what transhistorical plan or purpose sustains a people through times of nuclear annihilation, extermination camps, terrorist bombings, saturation bombing, and defoliation of human habitats? If we experience history as terror, we live at the edge of a despair, though we learn to normalize the dread through ritual and irony so that it does not tyrannize consciousness. (In North America we live not so much with political or ideological terror as with the self-terrorization of street violence, random massacres, gun-culture insanity generally and the contempt for public life that it entails.) Instead of a shared sense of transhistorical meaning, European and American cultures share a sense of democratic values meant to offer secular deliverance in the form of human rights, social organization, and that loving-kindness which was not so long ago Thomas Hardy's bedrock value in a world where metaphysics had been tumultuously undermined by Darwinism.

To identify the infidel then command one's subjects to kill him was, for the Ayatollah, a political act first and last, though the medium for that power was religious authority, just as in another epoch the infidel was identified and condemned by papal authority. Dante did not experience history as terror, because he believed that earthly events are, with the exception of the Incarnation, the results of human will acting freely while sanctioned and sponsored, however aloofly, by Divine Intelligence. Dante saw and denounced, however, the papacy's secular abuse of ecclesiastical authority and the corruption of divine office by political ideology. Christendom, he believed, needed a secular leader above all,

Shooting the Works

and also a pontiff sealed off from the political allure of worldly might. In *Prometheus Unbound*, Shelley says that consciousness occluded by power will lose the ability to imagine freedom:

> In each human heart terror survives
> The ravin it has gorged: the loftiest fear
> All that they would disdain to think were true:
> Hypocrisy and custom make their minds
> The fanes of many a worship, now outworn.
> They dare not devise good for man's estate,
> And yet they know not that they do not dare.
> The good want power, but to weep barren tears.
> The powerful goodness want: worse need for them.
> The wise want love; and those who love want wisdom;
> And all best things are thus confused to ill.

Laughter

How do poets respond to living in the terror of history? They live entirely in their moment, as Dante and Shelley did, and also live intensely the near memory of those justifications that once gave (and for believers still give) structure and purpose to horrible events. They exercise, indeed cultivate, skepticism toward authority, which survives largely by denying or shackling imagination. Sometimes the skepticism is expressed most intimately, as dismantlings or interrogations of poetry's authority of forms, its available conventions and received assumptions. Sometimes openly, as abrasive, blasphemous, chaotic humor. The Aristophanes of the *Thesmophoriazousai* was a deeply religious artist, though not a complacently pious one. Euripides is probably the most religious of the tragic poets (much more than he is the magisterial rationalist he is often made to seem) because his lyric skepticism questions the very way that consciousness interprets the relation between divine authority and human agency.

When government or rulership is sustained by appeals to religious loyalties, whether by the fundamentalist fanaticism of Islam under the Ayatollah or the moral blackmail of the American Presidency appealing to a bland, approving, Lincolnesque deity, those in power would have us believe that human good is served best by impersonality, beneficent coercion, and generalization about need and duty. Authority thus elevates law above embodiment, abstract generalization over individual recognitions, slogans over hunger cries. When writers like Rushdie suffer at the hands of a fanatic, it is because their views of reality and techniques for apprehending reality are not only different but contrary. The ideologue sees reality as a great unitary mass cohering in one idea; every nuance of change and difference must be answerable to the one idea that kneads all unlikeness into a conformist sum. The ideologue's technique is control, exercised as a right and a necessity. Poets who insist too much on a rectitude of forms or feelings or thoughts slight the unruly passion of difference and have gone over, to greater or lesser degree, to the mind of the ideologue.

And yet poets themselves are control freaks, because they have to govern their materials. But control is never the decisive act, and it is driven by anarchic mood that can send poetry spinning out of control at any time, into glossolalia or incoherence or looney tunes. The decisive act is form-finding, and that is not so much an act as an activity, a process of serial recognitions and discriminations. It cannot be predicted or prepared for except by the usual disciplines of candor, availability, and plasticity. Reality as an object and medium of knowledge for the poet exists not as something reducible to one big determinant idea; it is made up so much of phantasmagoria that it remains a field of uncertainty and weird promise. The poet explores the field, patient with ignorance and unknowing, resistant to coercive ideas and the sentimentalities of borrowed emotions. To the ideologue, to the fanatic, to the poet for whom rectitude and cautious illustration matter more than expressiveness, such patience will seem mere neurosis, a moral indecisiveness or irresoluteness, or a formal primitivism. Such patience is made up largely of laughter, an eruptive gaiety natural to the life of forms. Sometimes it's loon laughter, moonstruck, for poets generally do not care to be worldshakers but they work hard to make patterned words into a world of passion, of dense ancient amorous god-baiting passion. We laugh, moreover, at our own counterfeiting conceit. The poet's laughter, celebrative and giddy when moving in rhythms just now discovered, can turn enraged and petulant when the materials resist patterning.

Poets laugh—I mean, the *life of forms* laughs—at fanaticism and ideology by exercising the deliberative, nuanced pursuit of embodiment in language. Our true Paradise is the place in words where nothing looks quite like anything else yet all things together make one Paradise. Confronted with the poet's sticky hilarity, the ideologue becomes more humorless, more intolerant of moral surprise. We struggle so much with certainty (and sometimes even covet the certainty enjoyed by ideologues) because our work depends so much on taking exception, on moral surprise, on the trilled or mumbled initiating phrase: "What if . . . ?"

Uncertainty

Because I'm a laborious writer preoccupied by the dialectics of uncertainty in love and faith, I envy writers whose work seems voluble and casually decisive from the start and which, but for a little strain of adjustment and revision, seems a straight judicious shot from conception to execution. I don't take Yeats's assertion as a general rule of lyric verse, that a line must seem a moment's thought. Or rather, I believe that the process by which a moment's thought comes about should be worked into the textures of the statement itself. I recognize in the work of others a fluency I have never had, and that illusion makes it seem a real possibility. But even when the form-finding trouble is over, the fire damped down for the night, I feel agitated and unhappy, because of the uncertainty that the new silence, the quiet porch of the unimagined, will hold any promise of ignorance. For the imagination thrives on ignorance and on the moist moral impress it takes from new pressures of experience. I am happiest when I have begun something, when I have pitched into that homely chaos of formal possibility, when I do not know where I am or where I'm headed. It is a happiness like riding the subway after midnight. Anything can happen, and even if nothing does we will imagine some surprise or plot, a coincidence or ecstasy of patterns. In that zone of uncertainty, language feels like a treacherous ruin, and the task of making poetry, far from being a courtly or schoolish activity, seems one of elemental clarification, of dusting brittle vestiges of broken pots and bones in the hope of assembling something—history, fact, material, a feeling for what is just and beautiful—that might be made whole and true.

I read poems in books and magazines and am amazed by the ranging, assured, exquisitely toned sensibilities on display. Sometimes it's powerfully attractive, because it feels a world apart from my own cult of anxiety and laboriousness. I tell myself: One can tolerate only so much conflict in the textures of words. Quit fussing and say something plain. A friend gently reminds me: Isn't it possible to be both strong *and* clear?

I once heard someone, misquoting Keats, speak of "negative culpability." That is something morally original, and it has a useful sense. Fault in poetry is the broken seam where meaning can be found, the kind of meaning that cannot be anticipated but waits there. Lear's Fool tells the old fool that the nose sits in the middle of the face to set the eyes both sides of the nose, so that what we cannot smell out we may spy into. The critical moment is when I'm at the point of feeling nothing but the sheer plasticity of the words, when negative culpability itself drains away into the tidal switchings of the words. All the moral quality of statement breaks down into the voluptuous massiveness of color and sound. At that point, everything is at stake and nothing matters. Occasion, intent, and enforced shapeliness dissolve into a buzzing, marshy uncertainty. It's the moment when I reckon again that my attempt to write poetry, with all its halting correctiveness and will toward coherence, is of no consequence to the starry sky. To say something of consequence to another, or something which in the simple drift of its words gives a sensuous pinch or chill entirely of the moment, seems at once the best offering I can make and also just a (same old) beginning.

Ecstasy

I ask myself: What is the work of poetry? I find one answer in Ruskin:

> Labor is the contest of the life of man with an opposite;—the term "life" including his intellect, soul, and philosophical power, contending with question, difficulty, trial, or material force.
>
> [*Unto This Last*]

Ruskin was writing chiefly about manual labor, but with an eye also on intellectual and artistic activity. Somewhere else in his writings he remarks on the importance to a painter of physical strength and stamina, and Ruskin's own life as a critic was an illustration of the intellectual applications of his definition of labor. The way of contestation as a way of poetry has been familiar to me for a long time; it has also sustained me, too ably perhaps, for it can induce an arid purposefulness and a prideful certainty that contestation is the one true way.

I would stir into Ruskin's definition the quality of ecstasy, for the ecstasy of labor cannot be separated out from the confrontational elements he identifies—question, difficulty, trial, material force. Ecstasy is sometimes the effect of repeated actions, of serial exasperating trials, the recopying or revising of lines, the turning of the simplest phrase as if on a lathe, pulling it in and out of different shapes, newel post to broom handle. The mechanical action of recopying is physically keyed to this, and to the possibility of discovery through mistakes born from the boredom of the work. Ecstasy is induced as well by the intensity of finding the poetry in materials given or found—finding the poem in its occasion. It is the strange molecular displacement whereby we seem to be somehow an extract of ourselves suddenly come to life in a line or phrase, out of ourselves, out of the body, made over into language as if in a science-fiction cloning dream, a Golem in reverse.

Ecstasy is not happiness, which requires harmony, suitedness, a sense of untranslatable well-being, balance, and justification in the moment. Ecstasy is the child of excess and denial, of superfluity and poverty. Question, difficulty, and trial are its favorite companions and guides. On occasion it is a gift from nowhere, or from the Goddess, the housefly goddess on the windowsill. A line or phrase comes to mind, mostly already made, the finished fragment of a heavenly or diabolical script, and in that piece of language forged elsewhere you are momentarily out of yourself, out of your mind, at the mercy of the delirium of the gift.

Occasion

It is the initiating event, physical or mental. The starter. But the occasion can be so intensely lived through, physically and mentally, during the actual writing of a poem that it feels like something more comprehensive. It becomes diffused in the process of the writing, coextensive with the subject matter, worked into the plastic compound of words. Occasion—an anniversary, a battle, a recollection, the smell of a rose, the touch of a hand—is the single event that becomes the actual stirring of spirit toward recognition or understanding, the movement of words toward realization. A poet who assumes life goes on as an occasion for poetry has got the process backward. Existence does not need to demonstrate its usefulness or availability to us. It confuses me to hear people talk about "getting a poem out of" some experience, of squeezing from occasion the juice of sensibility. Existence is indeed an ongoing feast of occasions, but as I take my place at the board I hear William

James's fury and frustration coming from the far end, that he had to forge every sentence of the *Principles of Psychology* "in the teeth of irreducible and stubborn fact."

So occasion is not just an initiator, it is also the poem's medium, a squirming context for discovery. I think of it as a way of love, which is the desire to know the individual other. It is reality we want to know, and the way of love, which is constant movement, takes a poet behind what James calls the foreground of existence and reaches down "to that curious sense of the whole residual cosmos as an everlasting presence, intimate or alien, terrible or amusing, lovable or odious." Occasion pursued allows one to try to express the most particular, authentic, provisional answers to James's question: "What is the character of the universe in which we dwell?" It allows also for a common sense and public regard. Probing, adventuring, scrutinizing, making and unmaking, asserting and revising, these are some of the specific acts of mind that conduct a poet through the process of occasion. The inquiring soul, however it must paint the props and backdrops of the show it puts on in words, needs to stay in motion. The motion traces the desire to recognize origins and destiny in the homeliest and most abject particulars of life. If that motion stops, the soul dims and becomes merely reactive to the world's occasions, it seeks comfort in the protective coloring of mock prophecy or senatorial wisdom. Ortega says that love requires centrifugal motion, fleeing the center, so that one's spirit is "psychically in motion, en route *toward* an object and continually on the march from our inner being toward another." And that it is not a single discharge but a current, "a psychic radiation which proceeds from the lover to the beloved."

Occasion calls us to attention, and the plying of occasion is a current of sustained attention. Dante's physical movement through the three zones of attention in the *Divine Comedy* enacts the movement of his soul. He moves and, moving, comes to recognize. His action can be graphed as a current of energy. The initiating occasion is his coming into consciousness in the dark wood, dripping with uncertainty and the grief of concupiscence, which throughout his journey he will seek to smell out or spy into. The movement of love, in most poetry, begins with such an act of attention, often stunned or sudden, impaling consciousness on its own line of vision. The poet, the lyric poet especially, is Ortega's maniac: "The maniac is a man with an abnormal attention span." The quality of Dante's attention, the comprehensive intensity of his stare, is tested along the way. He listens, beckons, nods, quarrels, assents, chastises, and brings news. He looks too long on Master Adam beating the drum of his dropsical partner's belly and is scolded by Virgil for degrading the very act of looking. When the pilgrim descends to the floor of Cocytus, he sees souls frozen in the ice, filthily glittering travesties of attention doomed to stare down at the reflected image of their own corrupted wills. Dante accidentally kicks one, stubbing his own attention, reminding us that there are different species of maniacs. Those horrible figures in the ice exercise a useless, unchangeable self-attentive attention; they are emblems of the solipsistic melodrama so dear and close to lyric poets. For if the poet allows occasion to become prideful opportunity for mere self-display—self-display, so essential to lyric poetry—or a frame for obsessive loveless observation of detail, the poet's gaze may, like that of the traitors in the ice, freeze, locked downwards, our tears freezing in little icy arcs delicately bridging our eyes to the ground, the path of the solipsist's gaze.

Accident

Poetry is a constant mediation between will and fantasy. The will wants and seeks to contrive a certain arrangement of elements, bearing the burden of Iris Murdoch's remark that artists are pattern-makers. The will is procedural and conceptualizing; it can lead to overdetermined effects or canny maxims. Its hunger is real but programmatic and is satisfied finally by the sensation of coherent completion. The fantasy is prodigal, a mess of laughter, satyrish and dissolute—Harpo in his fright wig disguised as a cop. It welcomes extreme tones, actions without contexts, speaking in tongues, certainties gone up in smoke. Fantasy is not driven by desire, for it is too passive and recumbent to be driven to anything, though it is subject to a pathetic and maniacal excitability. Above all, it receives, often indiscriminately, and when serious deliberation begins— grave deliberations about moral quality, formal rectitude, dyspeptic dialectics, and definitions of terms—it wants nothing more than a long afternoon nap or strawberries with cream. Its voice is the languid, sleepy voice of the caterpillar smoking its hookah, asking a probing, curious, bound-for-certainty Alice: "Who are *you?*" Language, abstract as it is, is yet so sensuous and feels so much like pliable matter (and bears the thumbprint of temperament) that, in the service of fantasy, it sometimes desires nothing so much as its own pleasure, the delight of its own voluptuous densities, harmonies, unspooled vowel voodoo. The will, which really is a cop, wants not harmonies boiling over and margin-busting colorism, but coherence and resolution: every poem, for the will, is a case to be closed.

What does accident have to do with this? Accident may be gift or distraction, a wayward tone, a confabulation, something gone wrong, a wrecked phrase, a cry from the nursery that wants *into* the speech of the poem. Formal becomes floral. Error spills like life onto the will's hermetic soundstage. George Herbert's flower grows and *groans* toward heaven, because the sensuous tune of the poem takes him that way. And what sort of a man was Fragonard anyway, and does that answer anything? Accident can be induced, by breaking the spine of an established syntax in the hope of finding a different, richer, more destablilizing rhythm or structure. The relation of one object to another, of the eye to its motif, of the poet's self-consciousness in relation to them both, may be disturbed or changed by accident. When accident comes as a disruptive gift, the will welcomes it because it can seal a structure, complete a feeling—it aids in the necessary determination. To the fantasy, accident as gift or distraction is all the same. Let distraction lead me from what I thought a poem was becoming. Delinquency, wrong roads, wastes of time, superfluities, sketch after sketch and false start after false start, general vagrancy as part of the critical work of writing poetry—these are the things that fantasy values. Accident is another excuse not to go to work. Let chance meet the poem as it pursues its love, for chance may in the end do the most important work of all.

When I remind myself that the great thing is to keep the process in motion, I don't mean giving license to fantasy to determine the structure and sense of a poem. That is the proper task of the will. Poetry as pure fantasy would be poetry in which doors are constantly opening or closing, creatures coming and going, and under these conditions the act of attention, at least in my own experience, falters and dissipates. To keep the process in motion is to have the imagination restlessly mediating and blending, in all its plastic, image-forging industry, the directed passions of the will and the casual, extravagant, supercilious, dilatory, oblivious prolixity of fantasy. The act of tipping one smelly sulfuric beaker into another, testing the compounds, is the motion that keeps poetry alive and dense with surprise. Surprise for the poet, that is. Let poetry be entirely of accidental consequence for any person beyond its maker. Its surprise lives on, available for readers who turn to poetry not for curricular pedantries or workshop brillancies but for the plain promise of a language to embody the passion of consciousness, which is the ordinary work of the imagination. Alice tells the caterpillar that someday he will surely feel as strange as she does (she is only a few inches tall) when he turns into a chrysalis and then turns into a butterfly. "I should think," she says, "you'll feel it a little queer, wouldn't you?" And the caterpillar replies: "Not a bit."

Gots Is What You Got

"I GOTTA USE WORDS WHEN I TALK TO YOU."

"Sweeney Agonistes"

What are beginnings? A constantly melting and recomposing amalgam of images? A sentence we keep writing and revising? A messy album of meanings in which we seek patterns to explain to ourselves the mystery of personality? One of my favorite passages in Ruskin's *Praeterita* describes the soft orchestration of his family's voices:

> I never had heard my father's or mother's voice once raised in any question with each other, nor seen an angry, or even a slightly hurt or offended, glance in the eyes of either. I had never heard a servant scolded; nor even suddenly, passionately, or in any severe manner, blamed.

His household must have been a walled garden of mild manners. This to me is a powerful legend of childhood because it is so mysteriously remote from my own, which was charged with the electricity of blame, of real or presumed or anticipated offense. There were few mild manners in my family or in the immigrant neighborhood where I grew up. Mildness was a liability. In a boy, it attracted predators like a scent. Mildness could not be a chosen mood or humor; it was a flaw in the stone of personality, a symptom of sickness. A diffident, soft-spoken man like my father (who had breakdowns just like a friend of his, the only other mild-mannered man I remember from our circle of friends) was considered weak, inadequate, or disabled in spirit, though the nicety people used to conceal this conviction was to say he was (like his shattered friend) "a good man."

The voices of my world were seldom tender and unquestioning. Conversations, especially among members of my mother's family, were choleric eruptions. If by some accident a rational argument took place, defeat was registered not by words of acknowledgment but by a sardonic, defiant sneer. (We became masters as well of the mannered condescension Pope describes in "Epistle to Doctor Arbuthnot:" "And without sneering, teach the rest to sneer.") Anger, impatience, and dismissive ridicule of the unfamiliar were the most familiar moods. Everyone around me, it seemed, except for my father's side of the family, spoke in brittle, pugnacious tones that I still hear when my own voice comes snarling out of its vinegary corner. My neighbors, having no servants to scold, scolded one another instead. There were no degrees of criticism or disapproval, only a single absolute pitch of dismissal. I heard it from when I was a child until I was an adolescent, when my friend Joey T., a sweethearted boy who sat behind me in home room, enthusiastically offered to shoot a teacher (a priest) who had been tormenting me. A year earlier, he wanted to do the same to a boy who was bullying me: "I'll shoot the son of a bitch in the face!" Later, after I'd left South Philadelphia, I encountered the different sorts of polite, well-bred nastiness and intolerance practiced by other sorts of people, casually genteel protestant expressions of "displeasure" that made me nostalgic for the operatic candor of my own culture.

A loud disruptive tonality was also the medium for affection or delight, the way a shriek might indicate terror or frivolity. It was, in any case, not an excitability which people directed at one another. I hardly ever heard anyone in my family or neighborhood say they were angry with (or fond of) so-and-so. It was instead an aimless but earnest wrathfulness or rapture, theatrical and mostly purposeless, a kind of roving sparkiness going off constantly in the universe at large, for it also took in God and all His angels and His saints. My people always seemed to

Gots Is What You Got

be picking a fight with circumstance, with the very fact of circumstance, and in the absence of specific aggravating circumstance the cosmos would do. I did not know how strange or peculiar this was until I left it behind and found outside my culture a broader and more pliable medium for moral feeling. Nor did I realize how deeply its music had settled in my heart until I heard in my poetry that same extremity of unease and rage at circumstance.

The two sides of my family were the hemispheres of my own temperament. My mother's family, which set the dominant tone in our lives, came from a village near Naples whose name no one remembers, though my eldest aunt was born there and my grandparents, Carmela and Simone, lived there until their twenties. The Girone clan had the classic Neapolitan temperament, a volatile compound of hilarity, raucous grief, anger, and consternation over every one of life's details. It's a culture of sublime complaint, of rage or hysteria in the presence of divinely sponsored fate. Grandfather Simone, after emigrating to Philadelphia, worked off and on as a rough carpenter, drinking too much off and on, they say, and often drunkenly whipping his children with a belt strap, as he later menaced us grandchildren. His longest on-the-job stint took place underground, working along with hundreds of immigrant laborers to build the Philadelphia subway system. His wife died after giving birth to their sixth child. My mother, the third of four daughters, became responsible for the family, and when she married my father grandfather Simone came to live with them. He lived with us for many years, and when he died at ninety-three, gruffly attributing his age to robust bloodlines, dago red, and blackleaf stogies, he spoke maybe fifty words of English, many of them obscenities that sparked from his mouth whenever Eliot Ness and his archangels killed Italian gangsters on *The Untouchables*, Italian gangsters played by Greeks, black Irish, and Jews. One night, drunk and in uncharacteristic jolly spirits, he confided to me that in Italy he had once killed a man over an insult and spent time in jail. I never determined the truth of this. None of his children would confirm or deny it. "Oh," they said, "Pop says all sorts of crazy things."

The Di Piero side seemed a different country. In some sense it was a different country, given the distinct geographical identities of Italy's regions. The emotional and intellectual climate of the Di Piero hemisphere was so different that even now, thinking it, I feel it. The Neapolitan Girones were voluble, brash, impetuous, defiant, and proud of their toughness. The Abruzzese Di Pieros were reserved, quiet-spoken, self-contained, and they reflected more complexly on the particulars of experience. The Girones felt that too much thinking would make you crazy, complexity was a kind of sinfulness. Among the Girones I felt I was being watched, among the Di Pieros I was being seen. My father, his younger brother, and sister took after their mother, Maria, in being gentle reticent souls. I've visited the small hilltop town in Abruzzo called Castel Frentano where my father was born, and I recognize its landscape and the temper of its people from Silone's novels. The Abruzzesi, they say, are *fort' e' gentili*, strong and kind. Regional traits should not fit so snugly as that one fits the Di Pieros. Their laughter was different, small and almost diffident, less assaultive than Girone laughter. Different memory hoards, too. Both families were poor but managed to make decent lives in the New World after much hard work. Grandmother Maria, however, kept a store of knowledge about the old country, the crossing in steerage, her husband Aurelio who died just a few years after arriving in America, her own situation as a young widow speaking no English, three children to support, the years in a sweatshop, and all the rest. It was she who told me, sometimes only vaguely, of our ancestors: the priest who left his property to the prostitute who had given birth to his child; the Di Pieros who left for South America and started new families there without dissolving their first ones in Italy; the collateral masses of Di Pieros in Argentina and Brazil descendent from those ancestors; the gamblers and settlers and plantation tycoons among them.

Gots Is What You Got

The Girones were another immigrant mentality: they knew nothing about their past and seemed to prefer it that way. Grandfather Simone was the only one who could tell us anything, but the only story he ever told me was the one about the killing. For the Girones, I think the New World was a happy oblivion. For the Di Pieros there was some sense of the gleaming shadows of past lives. Even their way with language was worlds apart. Maria spoke real Italian, though with occasional dialect words, the swallowed vowel-endings of immigrant speech, and the southernish accent of Abruzzo. Simone spoke only dialect, and dialect is not conventional language spoken with slightly variant vocabulary and syntax, it is a different language. A Bolognese visiting Naples will understand very little, if anything, of a conversation in Neapolitan dialect. When, in my twenties, I finally learned Italian, I conversed happily with my grandmother and, when she was dying, wrote letters for her in Italian to her nieces and nephews and cousins in Abruzzo. When my grandfather was dying, we tried to communicate, but his dialect was as unintelligible to me as my standard Italian was to him.

In my house, the Girone temper dominated, and so relations were usually tense, disputatious, eroded by suspicion, resentment, and spleen. The sense of the world communicated to me by those voices was that contingency, the fact of living in the world only to die, *disputed* human presence. The most of bird life that I saw in South Philadelphia were starlings, grackles, pigeons, and sparrows hopping around sewer grates. Later on I began to love to watch the varieties of birds, because they are body sustained in a medium of apparent nothingness, at home there. Canada geese barking one fall morning in Vermont. A cardinal flashing in a snowy wood. A cuckoo calling outside a farmhouse in Calabria. The early morning starling screech in South Philadelphia. The lesson I absorbed from the rough vocal music of my childhood was that we cannot be entirely at home in the world because we have a consciousness that dreams of elsewheres, heavens and whatnot. Tenants, not stewards, of the world, and the world carries on like a miserly indifferent landlord.

From when I was very young I was attracted, with the call of what is sensually and intellectually elsewhere, to what Yeats called "sweet sounds together." When I began to read poetry, sheer tonal musicality was more important than subject matter. I read whatever I happened upon in the public library. Poe, Lindsay, Millay, Sandburg, the Byron of "The Prisoner of Chillon," some anthology pieces by Wordsworth and Whitman. Bits out of Homer and the Arthurian tales appealed to me most for the velocity of the narrative, the tidal progress of surge and arrest, and the pitch of the telling. In good time, I became aware of tonality as event and felt my way into the formal pliability of language. Whatever is authentic in my work is due to the crass commingling of that abstract sense of formal beauty with the given language textures and soul-conditions of my culture, though when I was struggling for postado-lescent intellectual and cultural independence, I of course believed I had to refine out the "crudities" of my culture. And yet I never did shed my tribal legacy of contrariness, the festive abrasiveness and chafing hilarity that even now I still at once love and cringe at. It took me some time to realize that abrasiveness, mineral grit, could be the kind of pumice stone that polishes a surface and gives shapely forms a chased gleam.

Love poems I've written sound so much like bitter, self-canceling dis-putes. (A woman once scolded me that I turn everything into a chore.) Many of my poems seem to me only half-emerged from mud, or they sound close to breaking apart on their own tonal irregularities and emo-tional uncertainty. One can, I suppose, develop tonal range and the pro-tocols of tonal display through study and imitation and craftiness, but I feel I've become a songbird bred to a particular register of tones. I have nothing in common with poets who practice the casual, bland, discur-sive evenness of the plain style. My own rhythms, this side of good breeding perhaps, are in speech and writing so much interrupted sequence, a nervous anxiety about the possibility of saying something straight and clear.

Sour exasperation, shrill gaiety, raspingly curt affection, these were

the registers most familiar to me. In my childhood, the words them-
selves were often not even English. Once I walked into our corner gro-
cery operated by a noble, solemn Calabrese named Gumbo. (Who
knows what Italian nickname that comic English sound violated?) It was
a Friday in Lent, baccalà was soaking in a basin outside, I was the only
customer, and Gumbo and his wife were arguing furiously. The wife
grabbed a can from a shelf and threatened to throw it at Gumbo's head.
Though I could understand bits of my grandparents' different languages,
I understood nothing of what Gumbo and his wife were shouting.
When I reported this to my mother—I was seven, I sneaked from the
store without interrupting the quarrel, shaking with fear not only of the
savage feelings displayed but of the unintelligibility of the language—
she explained how Gumbo and his wife weren't a good match and didn't
get along in the first place, and second, they spoke different dialects and
couldn't understand each other. He was Calabrese, she was from Aldilà.
When I asked where Aldilà was, she said somewhere up north. "Who
the hell knows? *Up there.*" Aldilà, so far as I know, is no place name. Or
only in a special sense. The prepositional phrase *al di là* means "beyond."
(*Al di là del fiume* = the other side of the river.) In Dante, it means the
beyond, heaven, a beatific elsewhere. Where, then, was Gumbo's wife
from? "Aldilà!" my mother and her sisters shouted at me, as if to increase
my understanding, pointing north.

North of where? Naples? South Philadelphia, which was for us the
center of the known world? Who the hell knows? I knew Gumbo and
his family well. He was great lover of horticulture in that rowhouse
neighborhood without plants and flowers. He once took me to Bar-
tram's Garden, where I nearly passed out from the powerful fragrances.
He spoke halting English. When he quarreled with his wife, who spoke
fluent English, the two of them always quarreled in their dialects. In
those intensest moments, they became foreigners to each other. To
communicate grievance and ferocity they relied entirely on tone, ges-
ture (that can of tomato paste!) and pitch. For most of the people I was

raised among, it was ferocity, real or theatrical, that mattered; that defiant energy was our way of meeting the world and pretending we were not subject to its harsh ministrations and unfair judgments. Sense, reason, logic, sequence, sounds strung together intelligibly or coherently or sweetly or gently—these were suspect, untrustworthy, often signs of the power that other forces (bureaucracies, governments, professional agencies, outsiders) exercised to the harm or humiliation of people like us.

In *Praeterita* Ruskin describes himself as a boy: "I already disliked growing older,—never expected to be wiser, and formed no more plans for the future than a little black silkworm does in the middle of its first mulberry leaf." In time, we lose the silkworm's constant appetitive present. Expectations grow in us the way language inflects itself into more complex verb tenses, and they become the fungus that corrodes the leaf. One of my soul's conditional tenses ("if only . . .") has always been to live the silkworm's moment, completely in the instant, but even to think that is an act of migratory mind, of the imagination making images of elsewheres. Bunting writes that the poet "lies with one to long for another." The present tense is the stolid, dispassionate judge and minister to the encroachments of the tempter, the "if only" or "what if" or "were it so." I've never felt the urgency of the issue we hear much of in recent years, that of the "marginality" of poetry in American culture. It's usually tied to certain traditional powers which poetry has presumably surrendered to other arts. I believe that the forms of poetry can still express, more completely and with more complexity than other media, feeling in time and feeling for time. Verb tenses mix, coalesce, bang, and sag. The senses reckoning with their local reality, the heart reckoning with the political relations noded therein and radiating therefrom— poetry makes these a right, fit matter of speech. To turn these energies into mere issues or "crises" is already to concede their incipient powers. It may also be an admission that poetry no longer wants or needs to

Gots Is What You Got

give voice to the passion of consciousness. The issue is not whether poetry is adequate to the task (though the question figures in harmless after-dinner speeches at poetry banquets) but the ways in which it goes about executing the task. For me, it's not by means of genteel manners and overrefined sensibility but by making the language of poetry a constant viewing or scanning of origins, with ongoing recognitions of reality layered in. Not local idiosyncratic origins, not local-color origins, but the beginnings of species consciousness as they are figured forth in local conditions, local cultures. The migratory passion of imagination, of image-making, burns in the instant.

When I was growing up, my ear trained only a little on the sounds of words in books, and mostly on the cadences and textures of language spoken around me. The idioms I heard, their racy patterns and fiery tonalities, were often only partly released from an Italian bedrock. Since nearly every adult and most of my playmates had at some time spoken some sort of Italian, the English we heard and used was a strangely colored flower sprung from sandy soil. The Neapolitan dialect the Girones spoke sounded eruptive and jabby. English words with Italianate endings tumbled from unintelligible dialect phrases. *Boifrendo* for "boyfriend." *Baccaus* for "back house" or bathroom, because before indoor plumbing the privy was always back of the house. English phrases sometimes translated Italian idioms. Women in my family still say "I'll give you eat" because it translates *ti do mangiare*. I heard a disapproving father threaten his postadolescent son, who was trying to raise a beard, with the hilariously ominous cry: "I'll break your face with that chin!" Italian sounds fused to English ones. English itself was a marshland of strange fogs and apparitions. Antsy, Esso, rumdumb, rock candy, coalbin. Tootsie pop sounded kin to tootsie brute, which was how people sounded out *Tu sei brutta* (too say BROOT-ah, pronounced instead as tootz ay BROOT), literally "You're ugly" but spoken as an endearment to children, like "Little funny face." The vulgarism *cazzo* (CAHTS-zo, "cock" or "prick," but used like "fuck," e.g. *Ma che cazzo fai* = What the fuck are you doing) was

Gots Is What You Got

pronounced *gahtz*. I heard it said a hundred times: You got gots is what you got. You don't have a goddamn thing.

The English I listened to, growing up in the 1950s—I remember it as listening, not hearing or overhearing—was one expression of the unstable, poorly bred vernacular which forty years earlier Henry James said would become the emergent language of the immigrant populations flooding American cities. It was a vitally impure, try-it-on language bearing the burrs and toothy surfaces of languages more or less left behind in Europe and eastern Russia, with regional dialects showing up as weird watermarks on those surfaces. The sentences I read in my schoolbooks were, by contrast to my neighborhood music, affectless and imperial. My language for poetry would as a consequence become an English more or less born somewhere else, but where? Its caustic and sometimes comic infusions came from dialects already half-forgotten or scrambled by official English. My feeling for idiomatic speech became studied, self-conscious. I feared the embarrassment of misspeaking an idiom or cracking a malapropism. I still have to pay attention when I use catch phrases, commonplaces, idiomatic turns of speech, for fear of getting them wrong and making some heart-rendering error. I still commit to memory and rehearse common turns of phrase I hear on the street. And so I've become a poet who seeks conversational normalcy and vigor in poetry the way one seeks out a distant constellation. My instinct is the still childish one of taking what is given in language and breaking it up into phonetic pieces, syllable amulets, each loaded with some nuance of actual or desired feeling and the pied, scattered clues of sense. The cunning of "Tell all the truth but tell it slant, / Success in circuit lies" is strategic. What happens when your *given* English is in many ways cock-eyed or skewed and draws force and complexity from that? The artifice most difficult to sustain is, for me, that of casual normalcy. The amiable knowing style of much contemporary poetry sounds to my ear as phoney as the King's English. (Perhaps it is, culturally and politically, the King's English of our time, official and self-assured, but that is a dif-

Gots Is What You Got

ferent question.) Working the language of poetry has therefore been for me a struggle to momentarily stabilize what is by nature and culture *off*, unstable, riddled with fabulous obscene errors.

My South Philadelphia language could be brutal, and it was to my heart the purest expression of unreason, awe, gaiety, solemnity, and discontent. But it was also an impoverished instrument for clear reasoning or exact description, it lived in my mind as an enemy of such activities—impatient, stupidly superstitious, intolerant of rational deliberation, suspicious of coherences and consistencies. It blended into its tones and rhythms a sense of the sacred. But *sacre* means both sacred and accursed. We spoke of physical and psychological sickness as if it were the presence of a god among us. This was felt especially with regard to mental disorders, which were carefully separated from other sicknesses. The young bachelor on my block who was epileptic, the woman who moved objects with the power of her mind, the girl who possessed second sight—they were holy presences. But a friend of my father, a workingman who had a nervous breakdown and who wept helplessly for days at the kitchen table before being finally hospitalized, was not sacred or possessed by the god. He was a pollution, shameful and scandalous, as if his disorder were that of blood spilled accidentally in purified precincts. Neighborly expressions of sympathy were ritualized conventions of speech meant to contain the menace, seal off the pollution. The word "sickness" had an aura of mysterious visitation and violation. The phrase "nervous exhaustion" (*esaurimento nervoso*: I learned the phrase in my twenties and have not forgotten it) signaled some degree of moral expulsion from the community. They should have said, and I would have been better off to hear, that his soul was sick or hurt or fatigued. Physical illness was attributable to divine intent, it was some kind of election and was fingered by deity. Nervous trouble was (and is still) a humiliation, not an affliction, because it was so entirely a human condition, or a sign of having been abandoned by the gods. When I began to find my way as a poet, I wanted to make poetry seem an awareness of the world lived along the nerves, but ministered to by the difficult clarities of reason and judgment. The blunt play and immediacy of my local language was given to me. I had to learn the rest.

· **II** ·

Restorations

When I visited the Church of Santa Maria del Carmine in Florence in 1985, the fresco cycle by Masolino, Masaccio, and Filippino Lippi in the Brancacci Chapel was sealed off behind green nets and scaffolding. A squashed, weepy light and muted voices were the signs of restorations still in progress. When the Chapel was finally reopened in 1990—the work began in 1984—the Italian press treated it with nearly the same attention and awe as it had treated Michelangelo's restored decorations in the Sistine Chapel, though without any of the polemics over methods and materials that had made the restorations in the Vatican so controversial. I'd seen the panels in the Brancacci Chapel many years ago when the colors were so fogged and the volumes so drained that the dimensions (and provocations) of Masaccio's contributions were thinned out to a phantasmal afterimage. It is powerfully evident in the restored murals that Masaccio was a heroic painter, maybe the first in western painting, not because of the scale and grandeur of his conception, but by the massive, earthy moral presence enacted in sacred story. His pictorial idiom is densely modeled, mineralized, resolute, yet quickened with a feeling for the actual and audacious in its expression of religious passion in the world.

The project was commissioned in 1423 by Felice Brancacci, a wealthy silk trader and prominent political figure in Florence. The job was given to Masolino, who took on Masaccio as his collaborator. Despite the difference in their ages—Masaccio was eighteen years younger—the two worked well together, sometimes painting different passages in the same panel. (They had already collaborated on a painting now in the Uffizi,

The Virgin and Child with St. Anne.) Masolino was an elegant late Gothic painter, and Masaccio, as the guide books say, was the first humanist realist. What this means is that the two painters produced differently felt pictorial responses to sacred history. Style is the realization and completion of feeling, and when a quattrocento artist like Masaccio constructs perspective depths in images, he is punching new dimensions into the space sponsored by divinity. The imaged world seems at once a more expansive medium of divine intelligence and also, because of the pressurized spaces created by illusionist depth, more humanly separate and self-defining.

The Adam and Eve in Masolino's *Temptation* are courtly, serene figures canopied by boughs of the Tree of Knowledge; the serpent is a muscular vine of green light winding up the tree, its radiant curly-headed female face suspended between the two sinners. Adam and Eve are gracefully affectless, weightless in the medium of Paradise, their feet barely grazing the fiction of a ground. Their gazes crisscross, directed at a nowhere beyond the picture plane. As physical creatures they are neutral, placid. Appetite, god-envy, petulance, the restlessness of too much happiness, may all be elements in Eden's atmosphere, but they are certainly not compounded in Masolino's figures. The innocence of Adam and Eve is palpable but looks like dreamy inconsequential curiosity.

In rebuilding the color planes and densities of the original frescos, the restorations have brought back to Masaccio's art a massiveness and voluminousness that make his *Expulsion*—the younger painter's answering image to his teacher's *Temptation*—an image of the change in the meaning of human existence. The First Ones, leaving the Golden Place, are deprived suddenly of stature, sight, buoyancy, curiosity, light. Adam's left leg, the first planted outside the garden gate, is inert and colossal, monumental in its eventfulness. Adam buries his head in his hands; his muscle-bound back is already a peasant's mulish implement. Eve's stumpy body cringes helplessly in an effort to cover her nakedness: panic and shame are one gesture. Her face is pinched in a cry of alarmed self-consciousness. That's the new terror, or rather the terror of the new humanism. Masaccio positions the red-gowned angel above and to the left of the pair, bulking out and pitching down upon them, deranging the compositional balance so pleasurably worked out in Masolino's *Temptation*. The salient balance in Masaccio's image is the parallelism of Adam's and Eve's extended legs: walking as effort, as labor and flight, is now their shared condition.

The collaborative shuffling involved in completing the decorations, which except for the *Temptation* and *Expulsion* dramatize scenes from the life of St. Peter, makes the Brancacci Chapel an index of historical forms. Masaccio had only half completed the large panel of St. Peter raising the son of Theophilus (the magistrate of Antioch who promised to free Peter from prison if he brought his son back to life) when in 1428 he left for Rome, where he died soon thereafter at the age of twenty-six. Sixty years later the panel was finished, and others were entirely executed by Filippino Lippi, who deftly worked in concert with the color registers and deployment of figures begun by Masaccio. The figures Filippino contributed to the crowd gathered at Peter's miracle, however, show a sinuous contouring and unstable mass that make the scene more radiant, but also more ahistorical and idea-ridden, than Masaccio's intenser, deeper volumed figures of Theophilus and Peter. The robust, almost surly countenance of one witness far right on the panel, staring out as if to dare us not to believe the event, is Masaccio's self-portrait. He might just as well be daring us not to believe the *painting* event. Behind him, in profile, stands a figure said to be modeled on Brunelleschi, whose analysis of perspective guided the younger painter in his construction of these scenes and of the vaulted depth of the grand *Trinity* fresco in the Church of Santa Maria Novella.

Masaccio depicts holy events as acts of witness. In the episode of Peter's shadow, which had the power to heal, falling on a youth with withered legs, the figures are alert to consequence. Each contrives a different disposition of witness, from the hopeful piety of the ragged commoner kneeling at Peter's side, and the panting wonder of the afflicted boy, to the fatigued gravity of Peter himself. Masaccio paints the world's pitiless givenness, the crimps, sags, and ripples of stone and dirt and flesh. The browns and golds that darken and fold back on themselves in Peter's gown draw us into the scene as if the scenic were itself the substance of creation. These effects become spookier because of the bumpy uneven pitch of the chapel wall that enlivens the textures like a protoplasmic membrane. Masaccio is unlike both his elder collaborator and his successor in that he painted the force of holy personality, of unearthly power articulated in and through the body. The sturdy young men in *St. Peter Baptizing the Neophytes* are not posing in God's eye. The one being baptized has a simian bulk and slope in his shoulders that immediately identifies him as a descendant of the Adam and Eve on the other wall. Another stands in line shivering, his abdominal muscles rippled and tensed with cold. Masaccio paints this purification ritual as the submission of awful physical power to the power of promise conferred by Baptism.

Here and throughout the Chapel Masaccio's art is unequivocally dimensioned in the world. His decorations are so distinctive in part because they have no fluttery concern with overdetermined effects. Space is not ornamental, as it is in Filippino's later additions; it's a vault or block of time, an element that sustains suffering in history. In *The Tribute Money*, the episode in which Christ pays a tax with coins that St. Peter finds in the mouth of a fish, the disciples are grouped around Christ to form not only a mass of endorsement and loyalty but also, because of the deft perspective scheme, a ring of regard around a leader. They all look preoccupied, fatigued, a little beaten up by the world: they have saintly brown-gold discs stuck to their heads, but they look like dockworkers or peasants, their cunning charged with the mania of conversion. These are not charismatic individuals. Peter looks already oppressed by the charge soon to befall him. Their worldliness, their being-in-the-world, is modeled on moral intent. Their seriousness, almost glassy-eyed with effort, is a self-sustaining mechanism of persuasion; it will carry them long and far because, like Masaccio's style, there's no hysteria in it. Their faith is planted like a natural thing, like the sparsely leafed trees Masaccio has painted into the rocky Tuscan landscape behind them.

I'm writing this in mid-February, when in any normal year Florence belongs mostly to Florentines. But it is also 1991, and the war in the Persian Gulf has kept away even tourists who would otherwise be here in low season. The local economy is suffering and people are concerned about the approaching Easter holiday, which initiates high season. I've been to the Uffizi and Pitti galleries in February before, but I've never until last week been in those rooms alone. Hotels are laying off staff, cancellations are running to ninety percent in some places, and restaurant owners say that even Italians are staying home, close to family and television. A few experts are saying that now is the ideal time for Florence to review its own identity and to devise a master plan for controlling the tourist populations that will surely return once the war is over. The dilemma, as always, is that the masses of visitors pump oxygen into the city economy even while they smother the place. Although the Piazza del Carmine outside the Brancacci Chapel is packed tight with cars as usual, there and in the adjacent pedestrian zone of the Piazza Santo Spirito, you can see the dimensions and definitions of the Florentine spaces Masaccio and others took as models. A few months from now, if the war ends, that won't be possible.

No major exhibitions are held this time of year. There are few exhibitions of any kind, in fact, though the Palazzo Medici Riccardi is hosting a small didactic show called Van Gogh and the Hague School that documents and illustrates the two years Van Gogh spent in the Hague in 1882–83. He had been there in the early 1870s, employed as a menial clerk for the art dealer Goupil. ("Two years of black misery and hard work," he wrote to Theo.) He then worked in the mission field among miners in the Borinage in Belgium, where around 1878 he began drawing. In 1880 he decided to make his life as an artist, spent a short time in Brussels, then returned home to Etten, where at Christmas in 1881 he quarreled so violently with his father that he was told to leave. Thus he ended up again in the Hague, which he would later describe as his second home.

The Hague already had an artistic identity. In the early 1870s painters like Anton Mauve, a senior eminence in Dutch painting and for a time Van Gogh's host and teacher, along with younger artists like Willem Maris, Jozef Israëls, Willem Roelofs, and Paul Gabriël were translating Barbizon *plein air*–ism into a northern idiom. (Roelofs and Israëls actually lived for a time in Barbizon.) By 1875 they were casually referred to as the Hague School, and it was this constellation of talents that the energetic, unformed, and no longer youthful Van Gogh entered. His first mission was to improve his drawing. He had really little choice in the matter, since he couldn't afford oil paints and didn't like watercolors. His letters to Theo percolate with enthusiasm for his contemporaries. "A painting by Mauve, Maris, or Israëls," he wrote, "expresses more, and more clearly, than does nature itself." The seventy works by the Hague School on display at the Palazzo Medici Riccardi, arranged around eighteen by Van Gogh, illustrate the lessons he learned about composition, structure, perspective, modeling, and figuration, but the arrangement also dramatizes the passionate oddnesses of Van Gogh's early work.

Van Gogh brought to his new vocation the reformist ardor and spirit of social witness from his years in the Borinage. When he was commissioned to produce a set of views of the Hague, then much in demand, the work he produced was so unmarketable that he got no further commissions: he was attracted to working-class neighborhoods, third-class waiting rooms, poorhouses, and other unofficial subjects. One watercolor from 1882 is a view of a ditch where women are hanging wash on a fenceline; all we see of the prosperous Hague is the backs of houses in the distance. Although Hague School painters produced numerous genre pictures of the poor, they are usually cozy and patronizing. Van Gogh was the only artist to represent working-class housing projects, thousands of which existed at the time (and in one of which lived Sien Hoornik, the prostitute who became his companion and model), but which remained otherwise undocumented until they were photographed in the early twentieth century.

Van Gogh toiled, with manic attentiveness, to make himself into an artist, and toil was one of his early themes. Laundry women, peat haulers, potato grubbers, fisherfolk, sand diggers, women at domestic tasks—these were the figures he drew during his Hague sojourn. Though he had given up his social-religious activism, that passion fueled his artistic training. He was not very interested in still life and, surprisingly, did not fancy himself much of a landscape painter. It was the figure that obsessed him. He sketched working people by choice and necessity, because he could not afford sitters' fees. His 1882 drawing *Sien Peeling Potatoes* is moving and unsentimental. Chinless, with large blocky hands, Sien is a homely person whose attraction is rendered in the concentrated devotion to her small task. The woman and her labor are not patronized by style. Van Gogh's earnest, rough-and-ready draftsmanship frees his subject into unexpected feeling tones. While he learned some of the analytical dynamics of drawing from studying the work of his contemporaries, he did not borrow their preoccupation with calculated effects.

From Anton Mauve he learned perhaps his first major lessons in pictorial construction and painterly technique. He was stunned by Mauve's *Fishing Boat on the Beach* not only for its structure—we see horses pulling a large boat toward us, fanning out across the picture plane—but also for the handling, the tumbling muscular textures of sand, the heavy pigment dabs of light dappling the horses. And Mauve's *Flock of Sheep in the Snow*, which suppresses the dramatic perspective of the other picture but uses the same organization by concentrating dark masses in the center of brightly colored ground, churns the paint into unlikely surfing effects of violet-white snow engulfing the sheep herd. Some of Van Gogh's other enthusiasms are not so self-evident. He aspired to the painterly effects of Théophile de Bock and H. J. van der Weele, though their work on exhibition here has few passages of grace. Their oil paintings are lumpily modeled, sluggish, and pedantic. In his letters Van Gogh hungrily and sometimes indiscriminately admires painterly effects, in large part because he was so anxious to work in oils. He called his drawing "painting in black and white."

He modeled his 1885 *Potato Eaters* on Israëls's genre scenes of poor families gathered around a frugal meal. The tones in Israëls's paintings are muted, almost buttery, and diffidently atmospheric. In 1902, when Van Gogh's reputation was growing, Israëls titled one of these scenes *Potato Eaters*. The rough garb and faces of Israëls's peasants, gathered around the common bowl, are done in long streaked purplish flesh tones. Their faces register fatigue and tedium, but they are so conventionalized and drearily moody that they lack character. His *Potato Eaters* is a well constructed, purposeful painting, but it has none of the frontal immediacy and rude intrusiveness of view that give Van Gogh's treatment of the subject its grotesque candor. Israëls paints spatial relations as demure, recondite atmospherics; in Van Gogh's painting, the brusque curtailments of space are expressions of communal appetite and want.

The face of the woman pouring coffee in Van Gogh's *Potato Eaters* translates the knobby melodramatic modeling of flesh in an engraving by M. W. Ridley called *The Miner*, which Van Gogh discovered in the English periodical *The Graphic*. He pored over back issues of the journal during his Hague years, and his many pencil drawings take over poses and structures he found in *Graphic* illustrations like H. Herkomer's *Old Age*, which depicts a mean settlement house for old women. He admired in these illustrations their starkness and clarity of draftsmanship, their panicked high relief; he also found, I think, the alert sympathetic witness to suffering and circumstance that he wanted to achieve in his own work. During his two years in the Hague he set out to make himself into a fairly conventional artist of social conscience and was intent on mastering conventional techniques which, as exercised by the Hague School, had no propulsive effect in the history of modern art. His genius was of a kind that put conventional technique and customary preoccupations to the task of overmastering themselves and being deranged by visionary desire.

Five years ago nearly half of Filippino Lippi's frescos in the Church of Santa Maria Novella's Strozzi Chapel were still behind wraps. Now that the restorations are finished, the entire space blazes with colors and crowds. It's the most dazzling and exasperating display in this city, where so much art conducts itself with stern, measured flamboyance. Filippino finished his contributions to the Brancacci project around 1482 and contracted in 1487 to decorate the chapel purchased by the wealthy banker Filippo Strozzi. He was ripe for the task. He trained as a young man with his father, Fra Filippo, and later worked with Botticelli, whose influence beams in Filippino's luminous, aggressively sharp drawing. Sometime around 1485, between the two major mural commissions, his work picked up some of Leonardo's softer, smoky colorism. The Strozzi assignment, however, brought his painting to a pitch of manic stylishness unlike anything he or any other Florentine artist had produced.

Filippino stipulated in his contract that he alone would execute all the figures and the major architectural motifs, leaving only small detail work to assistants. He knew that his formal signature lay in his figure drawing. One of the two main panels shows St. Philip exorcising a demon from the Temple of Mars in Hierapolis. The courtiers clustered on both sides of the Temple steps are a tumult of quivering garments and drooping heads registering nauseated dismay at the little knotted muscle of evil that has exploded from the altar porch. Filippino's signature is written out in the drenched, fringed hair, the bony brows knit by concern, the pearly skin tones and knobby anatomies. The architectural housing is feverishly elaborated. Pilasters and cornices are barnacled with shields, lances, masks, amphorae, flagpoles—all the *grotteschi* Filippino had seen in Rome at the excavations of the Golden House of Nero. The perspective modeling is wickedly adroit: Filippino curls some ornaments back around their columns while peeling others forward. On the opposite wall, in the scene of St. John the Evangelist reviving Drusiana, we see the same trembling, windswept pitch of figures in a crowd witnessing the miraculous event; but we also recognize here, as in St. John's martyrdom in one of the lunettes, figures brought over from the Brancacci murals. The slave stoking the fire under the pot in which St. John is cooking is a ringer for the figure assisting in St. Peter's crucifixion in the Brancacci.

The crowds gathered at Drusiana's miracle look as if they might slide right off the wall, but for all the raciness of the drawing and the strategic deployment of groups, the force of witness so palpable in the Brancacci decorations—not only in Masaccio's potent images but also in Filippino's own *Crucifixion of St. Peter*—has dissipated into titillating decorousness. Technique has become unapologetically its own primary and all-absorbing occasion. Whatever desire Filippino may have felt to express sacred event in human history shivers away in a formal hysteria. The intelligence housed in the human figure, so happily expressed in Filippino's superb 1486 *Apparition of the Virgin to St. Bernard* in the Badia, has lost its grounding. The playful trickster intelligence, smiling in the face of the angel that springs St. Peter from jail in one of Filippino's Brancacci panels, swims away with fluttery insouciance in the Strozzi murals. Filippino is sometimes called the first Mannerist, but even painters as idiosyncratic as Bronzino, Aspertini, and Parmigianino claim in their figuration a grounding and fatefulness of consciousness. Filippino approaches the end of his career—he died in 1504 at the age of forty-six—with a rush of sheer, weightless nuance and overrefined gesture from which all the stark voluminous heft of sacred story has been drained. Close by the Strozzi Chapel is Masaccio's *Trinity*, where the canny perspective plan, technically *all there* for us to see, understand, and carry with us into time, still has the force of a felt instant of eternity. In Filippino's murals across the way, perspective dynamics are a nervy exaltation of technique freed from all suspicions of transcendence.

In 1490, the Duke of Milan engaged his agent in Florence to scout for artists for a big project the Duke had in mind. The agent reported Filippino's work as having a "sweeter air" than Botticelli's (though not, he added, as much skill). That sweeter air, the clarity, delicacy, and grace of movement and line, binds all the elements in the sumptuous 1488 *Altarpiece of the Nerli Family* in the Church of Santo Spirito. But in the Strozzi that sweet air turns sickening. This makes it, for me at least, a place to love and hate, because its perfections both fulfill and mock its ambitions. The thrill of such plenitude—the restored reds, blues, and golds quiver across the intonaco—is the kind that induces a headiness of wild vacancies and voluptuous inconsequentiality. The murals are monument to a time in Renaissance art when religious sensation self-consciously became merely the instigating precedent for an aesthetic event. In their fervid confidence and indulgences, Filippino's frescos are grotesque shipwrecked beauties.

Big Bodies

Sometimes it seems that after the recent austerities of Minimalism and Conceptualism more painters than ever are using the human or animal figure as a subject. Part of the excitement stirred by Susan Rothenberg's work in the 1970s was due to her almost retrograde regard for the elemental magic of her favorite subject, horses. Eric Fischl, Francesco Clemente, and Sandro Chia all dwell on the figure with the kind of blatant erotic attention practiced by Picasso and de Kooning. I'm interested here not in painters like Fischl, or Francis Bacon and Lucian Freud, who are obsessed with flesh and the condition of enfleshment—Bacon's glittering skin tatters and blood sprays, Freud's bunched drapery of muscle and skin. I'm concerned instead with the big hefty figures with melted down features (or features that function as visual codes) which appear in the work of certain painters. This passion for bulk and large-framed bodies may be a response to the withering variety of physiognomic and stylized types shoved at us constantly by so many other media. If we watch television (even if it's only the evening news) or go to movies, if we look at all the forms of advertising that circumvent our lives, if we look at photography, our heads begin to buzz with the proliferating forms of image reproduction and image making that are, to some degree, competing presences for figure painters trying to find their own way.

Many painters now "do" the figure as if it were a purifying or chastening activity, as if to reduce figuration to a freshly seen set of elemental forms and thereby counter the hysteria of diversity and detail available in other kinds of image making. We can sometimes see the work of dismantling and the work of refiguring or reconstructing all happening at once.

The precedent for this, I think, is Cézanne's work of the late 1860s, when he was doing portraits with heavy loads of paint. In the thickly scaled, palette knife portraits of his uncle Dominique, for instance, we can see him dismantling the traditionally figured head *because* he was trying to paint it *up* in a way freshly responsive to his feelings. The extravagance of expression is indistinguishable from the severity and sternness of the desire. Both processes happen as one formal adventure. Certain contemporary European painters are working the same trouble, though they seem more obsessed with elemental, primitivist resolutions.

The French artist Michel Haas has done work in recent years that is interesting largely because it lays out the terms and dimension of the trouble. He recently produced a series of mixed media works on paper that depict large monotint shadows or silhouettes of humans and animals on a monochromatic ground. The paper is bubbled and chafed by the materials. The columnar, ropily-muscled, armless human figures, the dense heads without bodies, the bird forms that look like boiled shadows, all have the heroic dimensions of neo-Expressionist painting. Haas's pictures, in fact, have a furtiveness and studied angularity that remind me of Julian Schnabel's work, particularly of Schnabel's way of inviting you into a painting's sign-system only so that he can then kick you out. For younger painters, scale can seem a monster that must be slain. Scale can be measured by sheer size and melodramatic dimension, as in Anselm Kiefer's symbolical operatics. Or it can take its force not from the dimensioning of a composition but from the voluminousness of parts. Haas's mixed media works are not large, but the figures fill their space with an expansive dynamic bodiment. Mythic danger, anonymity, alienated featurelessness (the figures are all crackly textured, rock outlines), and formal invention wielded for its authoritarian force—these signature aspects of Haas's work narrow its range of feeling. His pictures have the baleful cavernous presence of dream figures, but like certain dream imagery they are frightening for their substance, not for their definition or features. They provide a kind of decorative histrionics proper to our time.

Big Bodies

113

In the mid-1960s, before he began making the hulking upside-down figures that became his signature form, the German artist Georg Baselitz was painting a series of pictures that he called "Heroes" or "New Types." They are full-length figures, frontal, one to a canvas, the canvasses themselves square and identically sized, and they represent human beings in different stages of civilized preparedness. A hunter, a peasant, a more or less modern-looking soldier (male or female), a shepherd, farmer, guerrilla, or rebel, suspended in a blank space that Baselitz decorates with culture objects that characterize the context: pitchforks, rifles, animal traps, knapsacks (sometimes sprouting paintbrushes), constellated with miniaturized landscapes, houses, manure carts, and other implements. The objects are stage props, pictorial shorthand for instruments of circumstance, tools of destiny. The figures themselves, far from being picturesque or heroized in any faux-historical way, look stodgy, inert, ornamented rather than shaped by their context. They are all barefoot and many have a hand or foot caught in a snare, which in one painting is ambiguously drawn to look like a *vagina dentata*.

These "New Types" look stunned and weary, the victims of whatever destiny has imprisoned them in these costumes and fitfully decorated spaces. The hero's pants are usually undone, and in at least one of them the genitals are exposed. The figures don't look feeble, though. They are squared off, bulky, stalwart, a bit zoned out but not inept or submissive. The figuration of the "Heroes" series is essentially semiotical. Each bit of cultural posturing or costuming is self-consciously proposed as a sign bearing some historical or political or psychological valence. Instead of being formally built up, which might allow an image to challenge its own determinations, its idea-riddenness, the images are conceptually pieced together. At least that is the feeling they convey. Baselitz makes the body and its spatial container, its dress, and its local culture objects into a text to be decoded. The "Heroes" are postmodernist image-texts, pictures to be read even before they are completely taken in as painted forms. The ingenuous presentation of the isolate figure on a mostly blank canvas gives the series a plaintive, slightly abused appearance. They pick up some of the suggestiveness of a national character that I often sense in other, younger German artists like Sigmar Polke and Kiefer, that of the exposed victim of historical accusation who suffers only barely suppressed rage for being made to suffer that conscience. It's not self-pity or exoneration. It's a rage *against* subject matter, against the inescapably oppressive contents of modern German conscience.

Although his work is hardly known in America, Alberto Savinio is one of Italy's most peculiar and compelling writers. His first work of fiction, the surrealistic *Hermaphrodito*, appeared in 1918, and he continued to produce novels, stories, plays, and essays (on travel, art, literature, opera, and history) through the 1940s. Savinio was a comedic culture-scavenger and an exquisite ironist; his writing had all the self-awareness and reflectiveness that would become the stock-in-trade of later writers like Italo Calvino and Umberto Eco. He was also a painter of moderate skill and articulate polemics. He was one of the theoreticians of Surrealism in Paris and Rome, and he supplied the key vocabulary for metaphysical painting in the 1920s. (His brother was Giorgio de Chirico.) In one of the essays in his little travelogue of Abruzzo, *Speaking to Clio* (1941), he describes a visit to the Etruscan tombs at Cerveteri with his four-and-a-half-year-old son Ruggero in tow. The custodian requires all visitors to sign the register, even the boy, who, his father sheepishly admits, is still illiterate:

> An advocate of symbols, the custodian regards a signature as a form of payment, and this new Charon is asking for the symbol of a symbol. Guided by his Papa's hand, Ruggero's tiny fist traces in the register the graph of a distant earthquake.

Ruggero Savinio grew up to become a skillful and interesting painter whose canvases bristle with so many self-aware preoccupations of postmodern culture and the oppressions of its past that, when I saw a show of his paintings a few years ago in New York, I felt as if I were overhearing ghostly quarrels between his father and uncle. Ruggero's paintings don't have the severe angular draftsmanship of de Chirico's. The pictures I saw contained large figures roughly and enthusiastically cobbled into their surrounding landscapes, not estranged from them or reduced to spectral residues. Savinio is as anxious to situate figures in dense, lumpy historical spaces as Baselitz is to suspend his images of the human in a field of sparse semiotic codes. In Savinio's pictures we see human figures in conversation near or within ruins of a vague, unidentifiable sort, with parts of the scene scrawled over with exclamations in French, English, and Italian. Solemn, hulking neo-Expressionist bodies occupy not really an ancient landscape but a pictorial idea of an ancient landscape, with rubble and broken columns scattered about. The words written across the images layer into the history of the picture a touristic pan-Europeanism. The words seem Savinio's way of layering graffiti culture into the culture of noble ruins. The compositions are sulfuric, the handling deft and eruptive. From one passage to another we never know quite what to expect.

Savinio's pictures have a passion and unrest that I don't find in either Haas's recent work or in Baselitz's "New Types," and yet all three strike me as artists of a certain time and mood, despite their different ages (Baselitz is roughly a generation older than the other two) and styles. The apocalyptic strain in Savinio's representation of ruins, along with the fatigued figures recumbent in those landscapes and the multilingual word salad tossed into the composition, finally imposes on the work a fairly restrictive iconographic agenda. There is no moral surprise in the imagery, though it presents itself as morally loaded imagery. There is surprise only in the handling of the paint. Something, at any rate, and I don't know what it is, seems to hold Savinio back from a madder, more radical treatment of the motif he keeps before his mind's eye, of that sublimely ruined antiquity—antiquity as yesterday afternoon. Though

Big Bodies

painted on a slightly smaller scale, Savinio's figures have the overstated physiognomies of Baselitz's heroes and Haas's animals and people. The homology can be broadened to include the hefty agonizers in Sandro Chia's work, and all of them derive the type from the ash-can titanism of Philip Guston's late work, and before that from the mannerist saints and heroes of the Caracci and Parmigianino. Maybe in the twilight of the century mannerist anxieties about the body, its dimensions of feeling and its quarrelsome relation to the space it occupies, have come down to haunt us all.

On Paul Resika

When Cézanne urged young artists to paint their way from nature into the Louvre, then out of the Louvre into nature again, he was describing how idiosyncratic feeling should be toughened, tried, then released into a freer expressiveness by its encounter with the history of forms. The engagement with the motif liberates an artist to push harder at the resolved idioms on display in museums. For a painter leaving the Louvre or the Metropolitan, the past is a concentrate of formal deliberations more or less successfully played out more or less yesterday. The more deliberate a strong painter's imitation of a predecessor, the more intense his own emotional signature, assuming the younger artist has the stamina to hold up under the pressure of past achievements. One pleasure of looking at contemporary painting lies in seeing how the structure of precedent—precedent's moonglow—is plied for fresh, eccentric feeling tones. The taking over of iconographic data, the "processing" of masterworks as archival facts, is familiar enough to us in the work of popular younger painters like David Salle, Sigmar Polke, Julian Schnabel, and others. The pleasure of recognition there, however, is mechanical and self-congratulatory. A more complete and more unstable pleasure comes when the sensuous thrill of a thing painted is indistinguishable from the artist's exertion to recapitulate, break down, derange, and absorb historically articulated means. That's also the confusing moment when we can't tell if an artist is a successor or an exemplar. It's usually an experience we can only know in retrospect, as some kind of historical consolation within an already familiar matrix: we feel lifted out of ourselves by Matisse's *Seated Riffian*, by a Fairfield Porter interior, by an Avery landscape. These days it can be hard to distinguish such excitement from the titillation of certain kinds of painting behavior, when an image is intended to work on us (or work us up) by the theatricality of its existence or by its shameless anxiety about how it will be received.

Paul Resika's work is so far from such theatricality and anxiety as to seem almost hermetic, though there is nothing esoteric or furtive about it. For many years he has pursued his formal adventures as a task of finding and expressing personal feeling—feeling, however, inseparable from the feeling for precedent, for the colorist tradition. An oil painting of dunes called *Sleeping Gypsy* (1980–82) is more than an homage to Rousseau's painting in the Museum of Modern Art. Resika's work lightly copies the structure of Rousseau's—above the dunes shines a full moon, the gypsy and lion are imaged as recumbent swirls nestled in sandy folds—but Resika's image has a mood entirely its own. The dunes are fluctuating, restless, almost animate presences, and the yellows, reds, and purples have a diluvial swell unlike anything in Rousseau. The entire canvas has a sunny, savage immediacy.

Manipulating pictorial space as if it were pure mass was one of the lessons taught at the Hans Hofmann School, where Resika studied in the late 1940s. Like other young painters of the time, he worked in a semi-abstract style that kept a recognizable motif while exercising the discoveries of post-war abstraction. He started painting as a boy—he was born in 1928 in New York and has lived there ever since—and must have had solid skills by his late teens. After the Hofmann School, feeling that he still lacked the classic technique that would let him paint confidently a hand or drapery, he went to Europe. After brief stays in Paris and Rome he settled for two years in Venice on the island of Giudecca. A few of the early canvases, those spared by a fire in 1971 that destroyed much of his early work, display not only the technical expertise he was acquiring in Italy but also his way of transmuting classical precedents. In a 1951 view of Santa Maria della Salute, the great floating church looks more robust and grounded, less like sea flora, than it does in most representations. It's framed off-center behind the masts of a small boat in the foreground, and the composition is clearly inspired by Carpaccio. Another early painting, the 1952 *Flour Carriers on the Giudecca*, has a muscular *contrapposto* energy modeled on Tintoretto. Since the 1960s Resika has concentrated on interiors, still lifes, occasional portraits, and, most frequently, landscape and seascape. The modern colorist tradition, from the School of Paris to the Americans Marsden Hartley and Milton Avery, exists as an available shadowlife in his work. He had kneaded that tradition into the form-making process, but he has also vaporized it with a new specificity and saturation of feeling. He has been guided by Cézanne's remark: "Painting from nature is not copying the object, it is realizing sensations."

In the past ten years most of his energies have gone into large views of the sea at Provincetown. A friend of mine speaks of the massive simplicity of Resika's 1980s paintings, and there's some truth in that. The work of the 1970s had a more flurried, cobbled brushwork and more excited braiding of color than the recent seascapes. *Fallen Trees, The Ramapo* (1977–78) has some passages laid in with the palette knife, others with light capillarial brushstrokes, and paintings like the 1974 *Self-Portrait* and the 1965 *Blair in Red* are made more by the wrist than by the arm. The recent marine paintings look simpler by contrast, more reduced and elemental. They also achieve a denser complexity of color and a thicker concentrate of feeling. These paintings of the last ten years, the work of a mature artist whose maturity has brought a wilder and more extravagant curiosity, are in a sense allegories of attention. Resika is paying attention to the natural motif and also to the transmutation of nature's colors, which takes on a necessity and order, a second nature, quite its own. Though he is stimulated by the image-enhancing (and image-deranging) powers of memory, Resika does not like to spend too much time indoors. He trusts color to speak its imperatives in memory, but he feels reassured when he has both color and motif speaking their two languages to him at once.

On Paul Resika

Remembrance may intensify an image, but it also destabilizes it. Some of Resika's recent paintings have that double action of resolution and insurrection. He uses color expressively, not semiotically or as an index of historical precedents. He uses paint to express the sublime, not to illustrate an idea of it. One of the pleasures of looking at his work is the way it remembers formal adventures—the uneasy serenity of Morandi's cylinders and cubes, the colorist hysteria of mountains and skies in Nolde, the plasticity of exposed canvas in Cézanne and Matisse—not displayed as histrionic gesture but internalized and reimagined according to the demands the painter feels. Sometimes Resika seems to work color just this side of the disastrous energies of chaos. He paints familiar motifs with an auroral candor, stating color as if it were the irreducible determining stuff of reality, as well as the heart's clearest response to nature.

In the early 1980s, for instance, Resika made a few pictures of a bull in a field. In *White Bull* (1984) the animal is affixed to a pasture of becalmed smoky orange; to the left is a stone building with a blue door. Bull and building are a nearly identical gray-blue white. Behind stand pearly mountains, plumped here and there like clouds. The values have the heraldic poise of mythic action stilled to a scene in consciousness. As if to tweak that composure, however, the composition pulls our attention two ways at once: bull and building are each off center, and the animal's head turns away from that inert middle. The picture looks like a momentary containment of the blustery energies in *Vermillion Sky* (*L'Allegro*) (1983), where a tree separates the bull and the structure, and the colors are convulsive: purple leafage oscillates and curves back on itself; blue mountains are broadly laid on in long parabolas that pick up the mauve tints of the tree as if streaming in the same colorist ecstasy. Twisting across the central zone is a stretch of greenery, a horizontal axis forming a stressful mediation between a shocking orange sky and an orange field that deepens toward the bottom of the composition to hot yellow–streaked vermilion. The one becalmed color patch in all this

On Paul Resika

turbulence (a chaos of joy? *un'allegria matta?*) is the black bull, a melancholic counterweight steadying the sulfuric energies surrounding it.

How much of a painter's memory is embedded in a pictorial structure? Resika spends summers in Provincetown and since 1984 has made a series of paintings of Provincetown Pier. The composition varies little from picture to picture: the pier accompanied by two structures, one long and rectangular, the other narrower, smaller. Sometimes a boat is moored there. Behind is a big dense sky which, like the pier, floats on the watery expanse. To my eye, Provincetown Pier looks nothing like the Venetian lagoon, except in Resika's paintings. Whatever his vantage point, he makes the cold Atlantic of the Cape seem a platform or scaffold on which the structures of human toil have come to rest. In *Provincetown Pier (Claude)* (1984–86) the construction of the small blue pier building, with streaks of the sky's bright orange bleeding through, is reminiscent of Cézanne's way of constructing color volumes. But just as that quotation takes shape in the mind's eye, it's broken down by Resika's more ecstatic, elemental handling. He loads paint with feeling tones that can be unpredictably mixed, even contradictory. The sunstruck, cadmium orange side of the building in that painting, for instance, is both sumptuous and vacuous; its trapezoidal form is positioned dead center and its color spreads and changes upward to compose a sky, though that intense chrome is nowhere else repeated. The center, in other words, pulls the rest of the painting together while it pushes all its elements apart. In *Red and Yellow Mast* (1984–86) the mast sticking up from the bottom of the canvas almost to the top, tilting a little, looks like a needle tensed in the meter of the painting. And yet that slight form with its dullish color somehow colonizes the entire scene. Many of Resika's paintings of the 1980s show traces of Ryder's phantasmagoric half-worlds, though Resika is a more corporeal, Antaean sort of painter. And although a mastering composure is evident in the construction of these paintings, they are not essays in serenity. The summery waters in them may often be stilled, but the colors and structures are not.

On Paul Resika

Even while the marine paintings of the late 1980s display an unstable energy state, Resika's concentration has a synthesizing force: he amasses the sensations the motif stirs in him, he does not atomize or fussily isolate them. This is why his work can jolt viewers; his sensation-loaded colorism creates its own massive space. In a 1989 picture called *Silent Pier* he paints the sky tawny orange, the buildings Prussian blue, the sea a leaden blue-green that releases the values found elsewhere in the picture. The formal dialogue between Resika and his subjects is a fluid and historically loaded one. To address the motif is to address the mystery of space and volume, and that address (or interrogation) is mediated by precedents. Resika is certainly aware of how tradition works its way, transformed, through him. In the way his painting treats the irreducibility of color volumes, for instance, he continues and adds to the work of Matisse, Dove, and Avery. From Canaletto he inherited the particular problem of the marine horizon. Resika's early ambition was to lower it, to pull the horizon down farther than Canaletto (who had Venice's help) had done. His commitment to figuration meant he couldn't simply void it, as the Abstract Expressionists did, or make the entire picture plane a color field horizon. Over time he pulled it down so far that it became the shelf on which the motif sat, like a still life composition on its table, and in a few paintings of the early 1990s he vaporizes it. When he challenges the horizon (that is, challenges Canaletto) he releases wilder and more volatile feeling tones; his vaporized horizons create a raw, dreamy storminess.

Resika works inside and outside, sometimes starting and finishing smallish oil paintings on the spot, in classic open-air fashion. Most of the pictures begun outside, though, are brought back to the studio to be worked up, sometimes completely made over. Others are pure memory pictures of outdoor scenes remembered in (and for) the studio, in which the formal passion driving the work is the recovery of the motif from oblivion. He likes the speed of open-air painting (he has produced many oil sketches *alla macchia* and has done many speedy gouaches of figures on a beach) and is careful not to retard that quickened life when he works on them in the studio. His exertions in the studio, however, are not part of the formal drama in the paintings. Resika's great misgiving about Giacometti is that he made everything look agonized. His own ambition seems to be to transform exertion into uncanny sublimities of color. We do not feel him struggling with the motif or engaged in primal contest with natural forms. His energies, if they were once combative, are no longer so. In some of the earlier work, he struggled with nature, with its bulk and energies, but in recent years the painting process has become something a bit different for him, a more internalized inquisitiveness of memory and invention. If some of the work from the early 1980s now seems a wrestling down of subjects into forms, his new painting is more a passionate coaxing of forms into existence. In the Provincetown pictures especially, we see a kind of painterly rhetoric of emergence. We follow the familiar motifs through their formal changes, the adjusted luminosities of color, the quivering tensions of volume and space, the contraction and expansion of objects in their fields.

The recent pictures seem possessed by an interrogating watchfulness, an availability and vigilant responsiveness to the motif as it emerges, a watchfulness indistinguishable from the energies of display. There is no furtiveness in Resika's pictures, no privileged points of view, and for all his impassioned engagement with historical problems given exclusively to painting, he does not play formalist games with the tradition. His love for the physical world is inseparable from the provocations of memory. The mediator, the secret agent, is desire. Resika paints light as if in desirous pursuit of its textures and temperatures. The pictures do not illustrate or describe light, they enact its imperious, changeful presence. The blue of a mountain, the green wall of a building, or an orange sky will look tight or solid or massive until we get closer; then they are all wrist, strangely buoyant and less stable. We can appreciate the deftness of certain passages—the haunted nuances of shadows on water, the stolid ropes and masts deployed across the picture plane, the dense pier buildings and Cape houses clustered against the vibrant space of sky or sea—but we also feel the pleasure of an entire structure held in robust coherence.

During the past few years Resika has been exploring a new motif, farmhouses with red-tiled roofs in the south of France, with trees growing alongside and other foliage foaming or drooping nearby. The roofs, beautifully drawn, look ritualized in their constancy by contrast with the looser greens splashing around and against them. We can feel the brushwork enacting the force of the green world pushing against the resolved, civilized lines of the houses. The new motif gives Resika the opportunity to create more complex spatial relations and more sumptuous feeling tones than he achieves in many of the marine paintings. I think he has found in the farmhouse pictures a more supple and responsive space. It is not, at any rate, nature that he paints, but the motif found in the natural world. "It doesn't really matter where you are," he says. A feeling or affinity for a particular place is, after all, mostly an ordinary hunger for forms.

Resika is the sort of painter for whom the encounter with formal problems is so intimately a part of the way he feels a scene and tries to find his way toward an adequate—which is to say visionary—copy, that the sensations are inevitably historical. Formal feeling, informed and complicated and beset by historical awareness, is made more, not less, original by the imaginal pressures to which the artist responds. Resika's paintings are an expression of one kind of modernist American sublime, where historical self-awareness becomes entirely engaged by the formal adventure *so that* it may be undermined, disrupted, transfigured by the emotional rawness and force of the artist's response to the facts of his own existence, to the nature that calls him to the task.

HOLD STILL
KEEP GOING

In his introduction to an American edition of his poems in 1920, D. H. Lawrence espoused a kind of poetry now familiar to all of us. He argued that traditional poetry has always been of two types, what he calls a poetry of the future, prophetic and ethereal, and a poetry of the past, summative and heavily textured. Both are crystalline, complete, finished, and infused with a sense of the eternal, formally exquisite, symmetrical, balanced, densely harmonious, made of "perfected bygone moments [and] perfected moments in the glimmering futurity." Against these, Lawrence advocates a poetry of the present, where there is "no perfection, no consummation, nothing finished." It is a poetry imitative not of the moon shining consummate and classic in a clear sky, but of the moon on the waters, wavering uncertainly on the tide. Such poetry registers the flashing feeling tones of the moment without regard for the judgment of eternity, and its finest instrument is free verse. Its essence is plasmic, and its passion is for immanence, not transcendence. "It has no satisfying stability," Lawrence says, "satisfying to those who like the immutable."

These remarks extend beyond poetry to include changes taking place in all the arts early in the century. By the time of Lawrence's essay, photography had already become the most available medium for catching the quick of the moment. It evolved, however, within traditional aesthetic definitions, the same definitions Lawrence was challenging. Beginning with the early experiments of William Henry Fox Talbot and the exalted views of Carleton Watkins, Francis Frith, and other pioneers, photography experienced a kind of fast-forward development out of an ancient matrix: it first had to recover and reprise, in very short time, a poetics of eternity before it could take up the modernist work of making a poetics of process and mutability. Even early street photography like Eugène Atget's had an aura and charm of the consummate, which was challenged by image makers such as Alfred Stieglitz, Walker Evans, and Dorothea Lange, who helped to introduce new destabilizing impurities into the older poetics of perfection. Robert Frank's first major contribution as a young artist was to make photographs that were the sort of instruments of the present that Lawrence anticipated. His particular achievement in *The Americans* in the 1950s was to break down the classicizing tendencies of straightforward photography (still visible certainly in the work of Evans) and drain them of the residues of eternity. In formal terms, the moon upon the waters claimed his passion more than the object in the sky. Ironically, by the end of the 1950s he had forged a style which itself would become conventional, with a consummate finish of its own.

In creating a true photography of the present in *The Americans*, Frank unintentionally made himself into an exemplar or classic case. For all its nonidealizing intent and its nonchalant disdain for transforming a supreme instant into a beautiful image, his work from the 1950s became a kind of historical shrine. Frank could not have foreseen that cultural circumstances would proclaim him a master for having made images that pulled down conventional notions of mastery. And so he faced a choice: to settle into the achievement, build on its foundations, and perhaps establish himself as a heroic presence like Edward Weston or Minor White; or to dismantle it, break down the achieved style, rattle the perfected imperfections. Frank is a superb still photographer whose instincts have always run somewhat against the grain of the medium. His great passions are motion and change. Immediately after *The Americans*, he completed another major project, "Bus Series." The contact sheets of the series seem to have been made by someone who wants to be making motion pictures but happens to have a 35mm camera in his hands. The bus is moving, he is moving, the scene before and around him is moving: Frank seems to be hunting that impossible moment when the stilled instant of the frame leaks into the flow of time. Lou Silverstein, art director at *The New York Times*, has said that the bus series was as far as anyone could go with still photography "without losing what are supposed to be basic visual rules" and that the pictures were a deliberate attempt by Frank "to see how far you could go before you've destroyed the canvas." While Frank did not destroy the canvas, he did abandon it. He spent the next fifteen years exclusively making motion pictures.

In the early 1970s he gradually began to make photographs once again, which challenged the sweetly melancholic street style of his early work and which had a new pitch and range of feeling. To viewers whose sense of the possibilities of vernacular photography was shaped by *The Americans*, the images he has made since the early 1970s are the work of an artist reinventing himself, pulling apart the now conventional precedents he himself established and making them over into an art that is denser, less cozy, and more precarious. This prompts a general question: When artists reinvent themselves, what of the past should or must be saved, what brought over into the new definitions? This provokes more local questions: Why is Frank's late work not as inviting as the early work? Why is its feeling tone so jarringly uneven? How has the artist who seemed so unselfconscious in *The Americans* become so roughed-up by raw self-awareness, and how is *that* kneaded into the plasticity of the new vision?

For artists, the past exists not only as an archive of experience but also as a style. The intensest private history is recovered in the formal structures and contents of images. Even the most finished pictures—a café jukebox glowing like radioactive material; a young couple swooning in a bumper car; a finny 1950s Cadillac offered like sacrifice upon an altar of gleaming concrete—live in an artist's consciousness not as pristine monuments of past glory but as the ordinary materials of daily awareness. Much of Frank's later work demonstrates how an artist disrupts old formations and restructures them in answer to changed emotional and formal needs. In an early self-portrait made in St. Louis in 1948, we see the photographer, hidden behind his camera, framed and reflected in a window. The city looms behind: a bridge, a dome, a vacant lot, cars, and brick buildings. It's a jumpy image, with shadowy definitions, an early example of what critics would later decry as Frank's poor technique. The image is a classic arrangement of the artist set in relation to his subject, the city, but destabilized, momentarily deranged. Roughly thirty-five years later, after the controversial investigations of *The Americans* and the subsequent work in film and video, Frank synthesized his past styles in a self-portrait in which he looks out from behind a videocam, still aloof, but alert with the passive, predatory attentiveness so crucial to good photographic art. In the 1948 St. Louis image he looks like a cubist figure embedded in his surroundings. In the later self-portrait, he is in a void, without a context, and the image is not jumpy but steamed and fluorescent, the image-maker making himself invisible before our eyes.

That self-portrait is one of five large color panels that comprise *Home Improvements*, photographs made from Frank's 1985 video of the same title. The matrix has changed from the bleak public space in the early picture to, in the *Home Improvements* self-portrait, a kind of studio cloister. The later photograph is deployed in relation to the other panels, which are classic by comparison: two portraits of family members, a landscape, an interior. *Home Improvements* is representative of a good deal of Frank's later work in that it dramatizes his own complicity in making images of a life. Two severe panels expose the most important people in his private life, his son, Pablo, and his second wife, June Leaf. The other two images expose extremities of place, his two locales: Mabou, Nova Scotia (land's end with its lovely desolation of snow on rocks) and New York City (a subway interior with its alarmed graffiti—SYMPTOMS   IT

WAS DARK). The most disturbing is the portrait of Pablo, who, we know from the *Home Improvements* video, has been institutionalized. The image, in the grim tones and merciless definition peculiar to video, is drained of life force. In no way cautionary or cozy (or exhibitionist), it is the clearest image of spiritual agony that Frank has ever made. The extreme foregrounding—Pablo's grand, handsome head turns slightly from us even as it heaves forward in the frame—creates an unsentimental candor that seems, as it sometimes must in photographic art, like cruelty. The enlargement dilates the video textures so that the support looks like open-weave canvas. An intimate subject, Pablo is turned into an image pushed nearly to abstraction, to public dissolution, by Frank's desire to achieve a precise level of distress. June's portrait, on the other hand, is annunciatory. She is a heroic presence because she appears so fearlessly available to the travails of experience. (We know from the video that she, too, has been hospitalized for surgery.) Both images show the way the human figure embodies suffering and change. The Mabou and New York panels fill in the configuration, representing the forces of circumstance that affect and sometimes determine embodiment. Frank gives the depthlessness of the video image a monumental form, but the monument is testimony to private disorder, struggle, and soul-making.

The way he uses video imagery says much about the ways and means of Frank's later work. After experimenting with video for several years, by the late 1980s he disliked it because it felt too personal. "[It] really picks up everything that is there," he says. What he means, I think, is that total exposure is not the same as personal or private art and that video, for all its inclusiveness, in its way is too superficially scrupulous and tends to flatten all the elements in a field to a single emotional valence. Video does not really *see* so much as it *vacuums* its subjects. Joy seems manic, driven, hysteric; sorrow becomes shamelessly hard-edged and spotless. It makes reality seem floodlit from the inside and records physical activity with crisp but phantasmal precision. It also lends itself very easily to harsh affectlessness (and consequently has become the medium of choice for many postmodern artists). In exploring the new technology he was testing for blind spots, soft areas where qualities inherent in video could be destabilized and made to release new expressive energies. Frank's displeasure with video caused him to complete only two major projects, *Home Improvements* and *C'est vrai* (1990), but when he makes photographs from video instants, or brings over into his photographic practice the lessons learned from his video experiments, he discovers new dimensions of feeling.

Frank is an artist who takes what is available, finds the chaos in it, then finds a way of using the chaos. Over the past twenty years he has often worked with Polaroids because they let him admit and manipulate disorder in ways that conventional film does not. He says they let him "destroy that image, that perfect image." That is, they free him to pursue in new ways the contrary ambition that has driven him since the early 1950s: to make something that is not a beautiful picture. Frank writes directly on the Polaroid negative, scratching notations and impulses. The picture registers what is outside, the stylus records what is inside. The entire image thus becomes an opaque membrane on which adversarial pressures imprint their meanings. The words are usually plain, elemental, sometimes to the point of ingenuousness. The writing cracks the composure, disrupting the composition. The results are complex and startling. In 1978, while hospitalized in Halifax, Frank made a series of Polaroids of another patient. In all but two the sunlight from the window swells into the room, bleaching objects and people. In the penultimate image, we see the patient, Mr. Lawson, in bed. In the final image, the bed is empty and the window cannot be seen. On these serial pictures Frank has scratched dates, times, memoranda ("Treatment Therapy"), feelings and tidings ("Goodbye Mr. Lawson"), slanting himself into the story, acknowledging his participation and his own fate. At the bottom appear his own and Mr. Lawson's hospital I.D. tags—homely signs of mortality.

Frank's excited treatment of Polaroids is also a strategy for working away from, but also *out of,* the beauty of his early style. One challenge has been to discover other, more unstable forms of counter-beauty. With the Polaroid process he has created effects that literally dislodge or blot compositional stabilities and melt or fracture the frame of the image. While pulling the film packet through the rollers—he uses an old Polaroid 195, a much-coveted model among some photographers— he plays with the negative, twisting and wriggling and hesitating in order to achieve a "wrong" look. As a result, edges and areas of the image appear abraded, raked, or watery. He begins to dismantle the resolved image before it develops, and he does so blindly. The method induces happy errors of disorder and chance, which then become part of his pictorial drama. In the 1950s Frank was criticized for bad technique because of the skewed axis, tilted horizons, irregular focus, and shabby lighting in some of his pictures. These qualities all contributed to a classic American style. In recent years he has honored that style by continuing to interrogate conventional composition and tonality.

The pursuit of a counter-beauty continues after the film is pulled from the camera. Frank is notorious for treating his negatives like last week's grocery lists—he handles prints just as casually—so that a negative is "worked," *exposed,* for a long time after the initial, sanctuary exposure in the camera. He cultivates a damaged beauty in order to bring into a strong compositional structure the decisive random impingements of the world. This is another expression of contrariness, his unwillingness to heroize decisive moments or seek transcendent effects. One reason he turned to motion pictures was that he wanted their commitment to sequence, process, consequence. His still photographs of recent years are a natural extension (and lesson learned) from that pursuit. The images now are not "taken" but carried out, and carried on. And the task has often been occasioned by personal turmoil, by death or the passings of seasons, friends, and places.

The actual effects of much of Frank's later work are more quickened and emotionally volatile, and also more reflective and ceremonial, than the early work. Sometimes he puts contrary feelings into an image with such aggrieved simplicity that the effects are angular and unsettling. When he writes I HATE YOU I LOVE YOU DONT FUCK WITH MOTHER NATURE, the assertions have a petulant simplicity, but the words fall upon charged images of the changing seasons and of snow-clogged window sills. We should not want artful words from a photographer any more than we want artful photography from a poet. What we get in Frank's pictures are panicked exclamations, news from the front lines, wild slogans and hilarious platitudes (SICK OF GOODBYS CURB THAT LUST). The pictures of the 1950s were also riddled with words—signs, posters, political slogans, tabloid hysterics—but those messages were found already laid into the scene. In the later pictures Frank lays into the grain of the image his own frantic, intimate declarations. It is his way of conversing with the process of forging images, making that exchange the very texture of experience.

The Americans made photography seem a constant pilgrimage to an undetermined but mysteriously critical destination. Every image was a little prayer to the need to stay in motion. Yet, over the years, the artist of the open road has become for the most part a studio artist, though this too has been strategic to undoing a master style and seeking new definitions. We can track Frank's development by following one of his primary subjects, his son, Pablo. In the early pictures we see Pablo mostly among the protective and instructive society of adults, with his mother or at Meyer Schapiro's knee, or studying a newspaper as if play-acting at adulthood. He is free at heart but, the pictures suggest, a child of contingency. His father seems to pick him up casually in the viewfinder, nested in a scene. Later, Pablo appears as a young man in the films *Conversations in Vermont* and *Life Dances On*, and in the video *Home Improvements*. He is no longer secure in a surrounding scene; he is a subject under scrutiny, a scrutiny that includes the relation between father and son, artist and subject. We witness the disorientation, the strained relation, the struggle to articulate feelings on both their parts, until finally in *Home Improvements* we see Pablo in the Psychiatric Treatment Center in the Bronx where his father visits and interviews him. A 1979 portrait shows him holding up books and magazines that declare his interest in UFOs, volcanoes, and meteors. (In those days he was preoccupied with violent interventions in the natural order; there is a moment of tender sympathy in *Life Dances On* when Pablo's girlfriend draws him out on these subjects.) The portrait is a classic pose, the sitter surrounded by objects suggestive of his nature, like books or weapons in a Renaissance portrait. Pablo's look of bemused defiance speaks to the relation between sitter and photographer. The sober sweetness of the 1950s images gives way to abrasive personal disclosure. Pablo's name and the date appear top and bottom in the image, scrawled on the negative, sometimes printed backward, like mirror-writing blazed on a tree. The figure does not embody motion or growth. He has a sullen intransigence, and the image bears no sense of happy past or consoling future. All suggestion of passage, of life on the go, has been suppressed; we see only an emotionally laden present. Frank, however, as usual saves something from the old style. The newsprint images framing Pablo have the blatancy and missionary appeal of the pamphlets, signs, and newspapers that flash out from *The Americans*. The issue, then and now, is deliverance. But deliverance from what and to what? In the early pictures those anonymous messages often expressed some wild, beleaguered hopefulness, and at least a public availability. In Pablo's portrait both are absent: he seems to have sucked into himself all the anxiety and foreboding that accompany the kind of speculation that surrounds him. The words, shrieking cosmic disturbance, are images of an interior which, despite the pictorial force of Pablo's mass of hair and beard blooming darkly against the white background, remains painfully remote and isolated.

Frank's late work is more brutally weathered by personal circumstance, its resolutions more challenged and precarious, than the early images. Some of his most conflicted images, however, are structured on traditional motifs. In a picture of flowers on a window sill (*Mabou*, 1979) one of the blooms is vital and brushed with light, another drooping, half-shut, with gloomy dark textures, and the third is wilted. Behind them, aloof and ceremonious, are small wooden figures, made to outlast the flowers but included in their penumbral light. The objects of nature and culture thus share the same illumination; the motif, shot from below, hovers high in the frame, like a shrine. The relative degrees of perishability represented in flowers and statues are summed up in one irreducible condition of nature, saved from that process by the act of representation. Reproduced in the 1989 edition of *The Lines of My Hand*, this image seems a mere accident of light existing at a pitch of visual uncertainty. The picture does not make an issue of that uncertainty but rather absorbs it into its formal language.

Since the death of his daughter, Andrea, in 1974, Frank has returned to this event many times and used the testimony of personal loss to test the limits of representation. For an artist of public sensibility, the cry of loss needs a ceremonious consistency so that private sorrow may have a public shape and not return to the chaos of its origins. One of the distinctions of Frank's late work, in fact, is the way it has redefined decorum. In a 1980 memorial image, he has printed the words POUR LA FILLE over a field of flowers. The flowers are shaken and blurred, both by the wind and by Frank's deliberate use of a slow shutter speed. Parts of the image are in focus, stilled into a stable bucolic moment; other areas, with their "wrong" look, are tossed by the passion of remembrance. The image, folding turmoil into quietude, dramatizes the way emotion recollected in tranquillity soon tortures the recollective soul. There is a stabbing assertiveness in this and other recent pictures. The garish mournfulness of images associated with Andrea display grief but do not invite us into their aura; they offer no welcoming, consoling gestures. This is part of the ceremoniousness of the late work generally, an aloofness that defines more acutely, and with a jagged intensity

HOLD STILL KEEP GOING

unequaled by anything in the early work, a disordered spirit and chaotic mood. (The moral intent of the late work is that it shall not be owned emotionally by viewers as readily as *The Americans* was owned.) Frank has always been a poet of happiness, but he has come to make art that answers to the unprincipled disruptors and destroyers of the prospect of joy. We can sometimes feel the force of will trying to overcome the impediments to happiness. The most ambiguous message he writes to himself on a photograph is LOOK OUT FOR HOPE.

Some artists seem to move from style to style, subject to subject, with processional willfulness. All the disorder of daily life has been absorbed or burned off. What Yeats called the bundle of accident and incoherence that sits down to breakfast has been transformed and compacted into resolute, necessary forms. Frank is not that kind of artist. He is a scrambler, and he delights in subverting his work's most resolute, confident formal patterns and putting his most exquisitely achieved effects at risk. He once said that his favorite picture from *The Americans* is the one of a black couple on a San Francisco hillside. What he likes most is the look of anger and insult on the man's face as he looks back at the photographer. The three figures facing the camera outdoors in *Gilles Groulx Pays a Visit, Mabou* are rugged shadows suddenly caught, like animals at night, by harsh frontal light. Their features are a little bleared, and they seem to have momentarily stepped forth from the dark Mabou horizon behind them. The simple domestic ceremony of the visit is rubbed raw by the setting and nature's elements. In this and other late pictures, Frank stirs up energy that tears at the consistencies of an image. The very surfaces of the *Gilles Groulx* imagery seem to create a rough weather of their own.

Some of Frank's strongest images are of his surroundings. Mabou's extremity makes it a station where nature's intensities shape the life of the spirit. Frank responds by making images of its seasonal moods and the shifting relation between land and sea. Sometimes the permeable and dissolving margins of his images seem like analogues to the marbled frontier between land and sea. In calm weather, the land is a clear margin defining the limits of one element and the beginning of another. At other times, we see the two turbulently mixed, their limits contested and confounded. (Confounding him as well: in *Home Improvements* June fondly corrects her husband when he mistakes sea foam for ice.) In *Mabou, 1977*, the upper left image shows what seems to be ice (or sea foam?) floating offshore, forming and dissolving; stenciled over the image is ANDREA, a talisman of remembrance. The word, so saturated with private agony, is an image of mortal extremity laid upon that other image of extremity. The right-hand panel shows the same seascape, but in thaw. Frank then disrupts the balanced pair of images by flopping and double-printing a snowy scene over the thaw, like a ghostly reminder or augury. In "Frost at Midnight," Coleridge says that the spirit interprets natural objects, their meanings and affects, according to its own mood. In several images of Mabou Frank positions himself as the Romantic in nature, but with all the exasperating (and potentially neutralizing but indispensable) self-consciousness of a late twentieth-century artist. His spirit becomes arbiter and interpreter of what is *out there*, and remembrance floods the image with the stark appearance of his daughter's name. But he is also self-aware of his own desire to appropriate what he cannot really possess. His sense of this inability is apparent in *Words*, a picture in which his own early images, or a sign bearing the letters W O R D S, dangle like forgotten laundry on a clothesline before the sea. The true reality is the background: the formless, moody, rhythmic but murderously unpredictable sea. It is the mastering changeful presence out of which the human impulse to make images originates.

Frank's most operatic works of the last twenty years are the companion pieces *Untitled* and *Mute/Blind*. To make *Untitled*, holes were drilled through a stack of early photographs. (In *Home Improvements* we watch Frank give directions to his friend Gunther Moses.) Then Frank bound them in wire like a rag bundle and spiked them to a plywood support.

The topmost image is a 1950 *corrida* photograph of a bull with a sword sticking out of its back. Beneath this junkyard memorial to his earlier self are displayed faded thermal stills from *Home Improvements*, among them spectral images of June, Pablo, a sheep, and the landscape outside Frank's house. *Mute/Blind* is composed of outtakes from the 1989 film *Hunter*, mostly numerous small pictures of a blind dog and a statue of a deer, ranked and aligned on the support like image shingles. Some have been manipulated so that the deer's eye oozes blue and red dyes. By mutilating his own pictures, Frank is also trying to lay to rest an uncontrollable energy and make it into a ruined monument. He is driving a stake through a no longer relevant great style, mangling its austere beauty so that its formal ordered patterns will not deflect the energies of chaos into repetitive (and lucrative) niceties. He is trying to slay certainty. That stack of prints represents an autobiographical structure to which he refuses to be held hostage. The *corrida* image itself is one of enabling violence, by which civilization breaks its enslavement to the minotaur and its tribute of flesh and blood. It is also one of the many photographs he has made of animals, from the slaughtered horse and sleeping pig of the late 1940s to the penny-picture display of the dog and deer in *Mute/Blind*. The story they tell is that human consciousness, for all its inebriating inclusiveness, tries but fails to recover (or even adequately represent) animal consciousness. Frank's images show how animals continue to be in the world but, so far as our own consciousness is concerned, less and less of the world. Our representations reveal us.

The message written across one of Frank's Mabou landscapes describes the gesture of driving a stake in *Untitled* and could serve as a legend for the late work generally: HOLD STILL   KEEP GOING. Frank's brooding on conventional motifs is charged with unrest and discontent. In his photographs he sticks close to home, either in Mabou or in his New York studio. We recognize the same views, scenes, and portrait subjects. Within these limits, however, he pushes technique into stranger registers of feeling and invention. When we examine the late work, we see the present moment at unrest and a kind of anti-stateliness. It is immanence with a vengeance, in an art form that is often the true child of immanence. There are no gradual advances in Frank's style, no "stages of development." His style, with its self-questionings and abrupt changes, follows evolutionary biases peculiar to its own systemic make-up.

Those biases allow him to be both summative and provisional. In the late work he plays with materials more liberally that ever before, testing the structural and serial possibilities of multi-panel imagery. He has also crushed the space between himself and his subjects, and he treats exposure time as a kind of spatial dimension. He is certainly less concerned with the anecdotal load of the image and more preoccupied with the relations between personal and public meanings. In his way, he has become a bit more literary, this photographer who so distrusts the adequacy of words. But he has also, early and late, made words (or verbal debris) part of a scene. Words actually become the scene in one of his most recent studio works, *Yellow Flower/Like a Dog*. Two side panels show tulips on a table: on the left, the words YELLOW FLOWER appear on the image; on the right, the blooms look faded and scratch marks spell out LIKE A DOG. The phrase appears also in the typescript that fills the central panel, and it recalls the closing moment of *The Trial* when Kafka's Joseph K. dies "like a dog." Then we remember that Frank's 1984 film *Hunter* was inspired in part by Kafka's story "The Hunter Gracchus," in which the hero voices Frank's poetics of the present: "I am here, more than that I do not know, further than that I cannot go." The mandate HOLD STILL KEEP GOING translates that statement. The manuscript in *Yellow Flower/Like a Dog* is a rough draft, an image of meaning-making in progress. Phrases in the script—His feeling like a dog running after Afraid to give up—have the stabbing immediacy of private counsel but are also efforts to make a complete, coherent statement. The panel's edges are runny and uncertain, its meanings literally held together, bound, by the side panels' clear, still, solid frontiers. By each

HOLD STILL KEEP GOING

bunch of tulips stands a small, crabby-looking "Old Man Cactus," a witty stand-in for the artist. The petals on the left have a fleshy translucence, and their dark stalks are intensely defined. The shadows the petals cast on the wall have a fastness and materiality more stable than that of the material petals themselves. Frank's intent, here and in the other late work, is to give formal expression to his love of the actual, but it is love defined by mature, stark criticism of the actual and of the sensuous present.

Frank made studio pictures throughout the 1970s and 1980s as if to seal off the sort of accident that the work of the late 1940s and 1950s so brilliantly included. However, he sets loose into that controlled environment the hyenas of subjectivity, and also, while working on assignment, has made images that come directly out of the straightforward public style of *The Americans*. These result from external occasions, not from subjective, self-generated occasions. We might have predicted the subjects that would attract him: American politics and overlooked American places. But he has not gamely recycled a proven style; he has thickened and intensified it with whatever knowledge and sharpened sense the years have given him. Frank has always been attracted by the festive disarray of American politics. His pictures of the 1956 Chicago convention are dyed into our collective imagination. Among the images he made of the 1984 Democratic convention in San Francisco is one of gay demonstrators, arrogant, flirtatious, exhibitionist, and politically assertive. It is a picture that, as a political configuration, pulls us two ways: we see the public self-definition and unity of a group discovering its political identity; we also see a kind of exclusionary self-interest, flamboyantly expressed, that rips the fabric of consensus politics. The image displays a distinctly post-1960s style of political expression. On assignment in Birmingham, Alabama, in 1990, Frank made images of youths slouched in TV seats in a bus terminal that pick up and continue the story of the four photographs from 1955 titled *In Front of High School, Port Gibson, Mississippi*, where a cluster of smiling boys taunt the photographer: "He must be a communist. He looks like one. Why don't you go to the other side of town and watch the niggers play?" The men in the bus terminal look disaffected, bored, doped out by the image-dispensing machine attached to their chairs. Out of the Birmingham assignment came another image that shows how a mature artist can take a set of familiar forms, then break them over our heads. A nude black prostitute in a hotel room is flanked on one side by her own hard shadow, and on the other by the seedy glow of a woman's face on the TV screen. Substance and shadow, reality and representation, flickering forms, flesh and circumstance—this image of the mortal present bears all the thematic force of the later work, though its language is more explicitly taken over from an earlier style. It is also Frank's testimony to himself, of his passion for seizing occasion and trying to make a true, adequate image of the present.

Seeker and Finder:
Minor White and Lee Friedlander

Every artist is a case history, but what an artist produces so eludes or skates across or thrives furtively beneath the facts of the case that the art remains in crucial ways unaccountable, essentially unreasonable, respondent to mysterious, idiosyncratic instincts for form. The most shrewdly crafted illusion of good biography is the presentation of instinct as self-aware deliberation—deliberation articulated in terms of formalist problem-solving, life data, or historical circumstance. We are all casual biographers whenever we try to get our minds around an artist, and we arrive at our self-serving accommodations by dressing unreason in a fiction clapped together of facts. We naturally want the manic moods of instinct to correspond to a containable version of the personhood of the artist. Yet at the same time, if the art too snugly fits the facts of the case, the artist may be accordingly reduced in our estimation. Coherent artists are seldom great ones, though I suspect our own desires sometimes draw us toward those we can sooner or later make out to seem agreeably perfect.

This, at any rate, was my own experience with Minor White, whose photographs for many years stunned me with their cultivated particulars, their febrile graphing of spiritual deliberation. No other modernist photographer, not even Edward Weston, could make isolated photographic instances such an intense deposit of sensuous and intellectual life. Over the years I had seen many of White's images, but only sporadically, in group exhibitions, books, and galleries. When I finally had the chance to see a large retrospective exhibition of his work, I was puzzled and distressed. Confronted with so many images, from his WPA work in the late 1930s to the color and black-and-white photographs he made a year before he died in 1975, I felt only twinges of the shocked attentiveness that many of the images once worked up in me, and I think it is because those epic serial exposures did not in the end make up the kind of alternate, diabolical, truer biography that I needed to displace the tidier, more pristine one I had already imagined. I don't mean to blame Minor White for my own critical debilities or selfishness, but the retrospective had the odd effect of diminishing his achievement, or at least of setting it in a much smaller, tighter frame. Images I greatly admired—the solarized *Vicinity of Naples, New York* (1955), with its aisle of vaporized poplars casting hard, laddered shadows across a country road, and *72 N. Union Street, Rochester* (1956), where the light of a plain kitchen interior has the spiritual immensity of Puritan expectation— seemed, in the context of the life's ambition, self-consciously representative or exemplary, like illustrations meant to accompany lecture notes. The fact of the case, that White was for most of his career a professional instructor of photography, began to bear down more heavily than before on the nature of the achievement.

By temperament White was unnervingly both a literalist and an aesthete, someone who valued Yankee bluntness, but who was also capable of velvet-glove preciosities and honeyed self-importance. His first love was poetry, which he began reading at an early age. His journals record an interest in Baudelaire, Eliot, Whitman, and Blake, and he wrote poems through most of his life. He called his journal entries "Memorable Fancies," after the prose bits that appear in Blake's "The Marriage of Heaven and Hell." But nowhere in his poems or in his remarks about poetry and poets does he show any sense of the plastic values of words, their etymological textures and tonal contrivances. He apparently sought in poetry a gnomic or homiletic wisdom. Its meanings for him lay entirely in its statements, its sentences, which he valued as if they were *objets d'art*. He seems not to have known that Blake's "Memorable

Fancies" were parodies of the self-privileging spiritual tourism in one of Emanuel Swedenborg's books.

White's interest in photography was more or less coordinate to his enthusiasms for poetry. It, too, became part of his quest for spiritual self-discovery. He dedicated himself to photography because he felt compelled to give visible form to spiritual need, to preserve creative evidence, to image a truth that might otherwise remain imageless. The same impulse drove him to be baptized into the Catholic Church when he was thirty-five. The aesthetic glamor of Roman liturgy was surely part of its appeal, but he was also attracted by the central mystery of Catholicism, the incarnation, Divine Word made flesh, sacred pattern converted into actual earthly image. But he became predictably restless and unsatisfied with the mediating presences of clergy and ritual, which interfered with his personal relation to deity. By 1950, ten years after his conversion, White had stopped practicing Roman Catholicism. The development of photographic technique went along with his desire for an unmediated reciprocity in his relation to the divine order. He could never really be satisfied with any orthodox scheme of redemption, for just as much as he wanted divine revelation, he wanted revelation of the self to the self. He sought a recognition of spiritual selfhood that would be, like many of his best photographs, at once a material opacity and a metaphysical transparency. The way from Roman Catholicism led him thereafter to Christian mysticism—one of his favorite sayings was Meister Eckhart's: "The eye with which I see God is the same eye with which God sees me"—and thereafter to the study of the I Ching, Zen, and, in his last years, Gurdjieff's philosophy of self-discovery.

Because he sought a unified life, White needed to make his photographic practice the worldly expression of the stages in his journey. The act of photography, of exposure, became a spiritual exercise that might lead to revelation. The conceptual apparatus available and suitable to this pursuit was Stieglitz's theory of equivalence, which was a formative influence early in White's career in the mid-1940s, and which remained

Seeker and Finder: Minor White and Lee Friedlander

144

a constant, if less determinant, force throughout his life. Stieglitz brought to photography an article of faith of the School of Paris: Paint not the thing but the emotion the thing stirs in you; make not a representation of reality but an "image" of it. In these terms the purest ambition of photographic art is to give external structure—in the minutest inflections of tone, texture, and composition—to the emotion experienced by the photographer. Subject matter was more or less just a volatile pretext or occasion. The image was not a referent or exemplification of feeling; it was its equivalent found among the world's available scenes, then technically worked into a right, correspondent visual pitch. As White adapted Stieglitz's theory, the image would ideally become the most complete and coherent act of harmonious reciprocity an artist could make in answer to the givenness of existence.

Theory and execution, however, were sometimes in conflict. In 1947 White wrote that the camera "is first a means of self-discovery and then a means of self-growth. The artist has one thing to say—himself." This conviction changed very little during his long career. Photography would be essentially self-disclosure and necessarily didactic: the artist does not simply *say* himself, he *instructs* himself and exhibits that pedagogy in photographs. The actual expression of this ambition, however, White felt to be theatrical. The unified, candid personality that photography would help both to create and to disclose was inseparable from the machinery of artifice, contrivance, costume, and maskery. He modeled the manual on photography that he wrote in 1945 (the unpublished "Eight Lessons in Photography") on Richard Boleslavsky's *Acting: The First Six Lessons*. Boleslavsky's book stressed the importance of costume, the theatrical presentation (or representation) of the body, and this convinced White that the clothing of naked emotion was essential to photographic art. While he wanted images to be acts of revelation of the self to the self, he did not want them to be, as Robert Lowell once said of poetry, "meathooked from the living steer." Costuming, then, was a form-giving or transformative necessity: disclosure was mediated by artfulness. Only then could the artist's feeling pass from the private to the public space, from what he termed the merely "expressive" to the truly "creative."

This is important because, as a young man in the 1930s and early 1940s, White was essentially a straightforward documentary photographer, working mostly for the Works Progress Administration. Even more important are two soul facts: White's homosexuality, along with the social costuming and psychic irresoluteness that for him were inseparable from it; and his search for a sustaining religious practice. His life was a trial of conversion, in William James's sense of conversion as a restoration of completeness, the healing or making whole of a divided soul. We know from his journals and from the testimony of friends that, while he led an active and satisfying sex life, he suffered a constant agony of conscience over his homosexuality. In his work, the theory of equivalence was one avenue of conversion insofar as it held out the possibility of a photograph being a whole metaphor of spirit, a harmonious correspondence. White took the possibility of equivalence further than the secular-minded Stieglitz could have imagined, maintaining that an image could be a realization of the Taoist assertion, "As in heaven, so on earth." He came to believe that "creative" photography was an attempt to align spirit, self, and world. "Spirit selects its own photographer," he wrote. "All we can do is to be open to Spirit." Many of White's admirers find in his images confirmation of this purity of purpose. To me, his spirituality, as expressed in the images and enacted in his life, seems arch, willful, and self-satisfied—the sort of rogue spirituality all too familiar in our desacralized time.

White in fact may be an exemplar of the kind of postwar American artist who could not do without a belief system but who, in a time such as ours, was condemned to spiritual nomadism, a migratory anxiety that drove him from one spiritual discipline to another. I understand very well that anxiety, and I admire White's stamina as a seeker, but I think his quest was in part misconceived. Unless artists exist in a religiously unified society that confers on them sacred image-making duties, which may also overlap with the healing offices of the shaman or medicine man, their work will be priestly or liturgical only figuratively, because its authority and sponsorship lie entirely in the self or in a formal tradition. American artists have for a long time now been spiritually disenfranchised, unhoused, unsponsored, and unaccommodated (though there are the popular nostalgists of religious homogeneity who would have us believe that to wish for sacred sponsorship and sacred tribal unities is to make them exist), and in those circumstances artists willing to answer to the sensed presence of the sacred must do so in the wilderness of consciousness. My own feeling is that artists encounter the sacred by worshipping at the world's shrine, and its idol is consciousness, within which live the meaning and value of transcendence. The terror Minor White felt, I believe, was that of making sacred art without himself having a sustaining medium of belief. In a sense, the classroom became his church and his students his fellow acolytes. His manner, certainly in his art and reportedly in his person as well, was mostly pacifist and benign, not contentious or pugnacious, perhaps because his quest was not to know or recognize the face of God, but to reveal spirit. He was a peculiar sort of Western artist in that he wanted to make available in an image a spiritual condition or state, not a divine form or shape.

White held firmly to the belief that transcendence and immanence may be "aligned" in the photographer and in the photographer's work. Just as important as the decisive moment when the shutter is released, and as important as the process of resubstantiating the world when positives are made from negatives, was the soul's discipline of self-preparedness, the ritualized priming of the spirit to commit an act of image-making. Sometime in the 1960s he wrote a poem: "When the photograph is a mirror / of the man / and the man is a mirror of the world / then Spirit might take over." This is an odd sentiment coming from a modernist photographer, not only because of the high finish and calculated "costuming" of his pictures, but also because his obsession with harmonies originating beyond the image, beyond material existence, but converging on the ground glass—alignments, mirror fusions, coherences, and coalescences—runs contrary to the ordinary powers of photography to differentiate, atomize, separate, and set at odds. Sometimes we do feel the force of unlikeness, as in *The Three Thirds* (1957), an image of a weather-worn side of a country building whose two windows, one intact and reflecting a cloudy sky, the other shattered and jagged, balance like scales on both sides of a boarded-up opening where beads of caulking ooze into the light. And in such male portraits as *Mark Adams* (1950) and *Arlington* (1973), White could be a moody sensualist and make us feel erotic force condensed into material presence.

But in so many others, especially in the New York and Vermont pictures of icicles and snow-glyphs, and in his images of the sea and sky and rocks of the West Coast, the consistencies of material reality are tenuous, porous, a momentary webby membrane where immanent presences fuse to some mysterious, constant transcendent power. Or, to use White's own term, the ecstasy of recognition felt by the image-maker is "costumed" in that fusion, that scenic contrivance. His extraordinary images of frost on windowpanes are palimpsests, writings over writings, the language of photography laid on the language placed by nature roughly and haphazardly before us: the resolution of both constitutes the writing of the artist. These images are perfect "alignments," and it is White's distinction to have produced images of such intense formal resolution while practicing photography as a religious habit. Sometimes his fervor reached an evangelical pitch. "Art is a communication of ecstasy," he wrote in 1950, "it is one of the faiths of man. For all my photographing the lonely, the frustrated, the despair, it is my belief that my aim with art is the solution of these things within the work of art." Unlike other photographers of his generation, whose methods he learned and practiced (he was a great admirer and friend of Weston), White intended his images to be of use, and their use was deliverance.

And yet out of this came a life's work that does not exhibit the processional formal redefinitions, the expansive testing of the plasticity of the image, or the encyclopedic passion to exhaust subject matter that we see in the work of his contemporaries. Of all the moderns it was he who wrote and lectured most about art as seeking, struggle, inquiry, and ecstasy, but whose images show only the slightest signs of those exertions, perhaps because of the oriental cast of thought that began to dominate his work in the late 1950s. In a journal entry written in 1958, White describes the moment of exposure not as a "supreme instant," as Weston and Stieglitz understood it—when the past, present, and future of the photographer interfuse as a sort of exponential intensification of personality—but as a Zen moment, a "no-mind" act (and not even so much an act as a condition of being) in which Spirit takes over. When the traditional Western relations between subject and object break down in this way, the act of seeking no longer seems like *pursuit*. While he owed much to the technical breakthroughs of other photographers, and while Stieglitz's theory of equivalence was a formative influence, White altered in his work the philosophical dispositions that determined much modern photography.

Major recent exhibitions of other photographers—the Weston retrospective "Supreme Instants," Robert Frank's "From New York to Nova Scotia," the fiftieth anniversary show of Walker Evans's "American Photographs," and the Lee Friedlander retrospective "Like a One-Eyed Cat"—are ruled by an appetitive, form-interrogating, and always slightly impersonal restlessness. The handling of forms and pursuit of subject matter in these artists is so pitiless and ungenteel—I think of Weston's luscious cutaway views of artichokes, kale, and onions, or Walker Evans's visually stifling image of a penny picture display—that they feel at once febrile and imperious, nervously blatant and pridefully remote. These feeling-tones are bound up in the subject-object relation that White tried to break down. It takes nothing from the vitality, formal invention, and meditative energy of his work to say that, when seen in quantity and variety, from the early views of Portland and San Francisco

Seeker and Finder: Minor White and Lee Friedlander

streets to the late nature studies and portraits, it does not have that kind of unsettling effect. Those others tease us into thought. White's purpose was, I think, to erase the self-aware patterns of thinking's habits. One of the great images of this kind is *Windowsill Daydreaming* (1958), a picture-meditation in which the material laminates of a familiar domestic scene—light shining through a window onto a windowsill and cur-tain—become overlapping veils of light-shot air, veils that themselves compose a shrine: try to part them and you find that they *are* what they conceal. The wafered light and shadow on the windowsill and shifting curtain compose a familiarity and alienness that we experience only in places we know best. The image converts the insidious and necessary distinction between the viewing mind and the object of its view into a "no-mind" oneness.

White was very caught up by hiddenness and invisibility, but his images are not recondite or creepy or evasive. (If anything, they tend to become too illustrative of the meditative mind he sought.) He wanted the real within the real. In 1956 he wrote in his journal that he was seek-ing "not things as they are but what else they are, those objective pat-terns of tensions beneath surface experiences, which are also true." His ideal was that a photographer, in reporting what something *might* be, should invent as a painter invents, making images that "depend so little on the object photographed as to be (for all practical purposes) an orig-inal source of experience." This is his significant advance on Stieglitz's theory, which was too allegorizing (or too occidental) for White's pur-poses and which set spiritual condition in too literal or inflexible a rela-tion to the photographic image. White wanted to make available to photography's imperious literalism a dimension of annunciatory possi-bility, of a constant *else-ness* inherent in the visible order. In the overhead view of dunes in *Eel Creek, Oregon, 1966*, carved from the sandy slopes and hollows are shadows that peel away from the dunes and seem airborne presences. One shadow suggests a dove's wing; behind it lie other larval shapes, of the head, beak, and shoulders of a bird in flight. The textures are combed and stiffened so that the shadows are immediately only what they are—patches of blocked sunlight—and just as immediately they are emergent figures of flight, of animal existence. In a few of the images of frost on windowpanes from White's time in Rochester in the 1950s, the dots and filaments and scrims of ice look like acid figures burned into metal sheets. He makes photography's labors of light seem a corrosive action, as if mimicking the corrosive lost-wax process Blake used to engrave "The Marriage of Heaven and Hell."

Early in the century, Eugène Atget went around photographing Paris's commercial districts, making images of the new organizations of consumer goods. His images of shop windows crammed with products, staging areas for emergent capitalist abundance, became a model for subsequent photographers of commercial life. Lee Friedlander began to attract attention as a straightforward photographer in the early 1960s, working out of the tradition of Walker Evans and Robert Frank. He declared then that he was trying to photograph "the American social landscape and its conditions." His many pictures of storefronts and shop windows recapitulate Atget's enterprise with an American difference. Atget found a new world of material prosperity seated in the old economic and cultural formations of Second Empire France. Friedlander's field of vision is not a cornucopia of wares and products; his window displays are pristine zones of absences and destitutions, Puritan denial housed in spaces fitted for material satisfactions. As display cases of advanced civilization, they mark an aging, nearly depleted commercial vitality. Friedlander presents these visions with no mockery or smug critical agenda. What seems to interest him is the proliferation of reflective surfaces that pick up, record, and bounce back at us not only the spectral residues of the objects of desire on display, but also laminar reflections of spectators, window dressers, passers-by, proprietors, and sometimes Friedlander himself, the artist-haunter. His window scenes usurp more of life's vitality and debris, and more of self-consciousness, than Atget ever dreamed of. When he imprints his own image on those glass pools, he is Narcissus camouflaged by an image-producing machine, fixing himself to the serial images on the glass (and making his own contribution to one kind of mass reproduction).

While Atget sought a massive density of textures in those shop windows filled with suits, corsets, or shoes, Friedlander gives us a sheeted porousness, the outside seeping in. He layers the given scene with scrims of light, like sheets of clear oil bearing alien images. His pictures enact the filminess of film—film as image-adhesive. In *Washington D. C.*, 1962, the photographer's reflection is visible on a window behind which appear a sign ("CARRY OUT ORDERS"), a tall vase of roses, and a portrait of John and Jackie Kennedy. The ceremonialism of portrait and flowers tumbles with the commercial message-jolt, producing a peculiarly American tonality: the respectful and hopeful enshrinement of the First Family is folded right into the texture of grabby marketing. The photographer's figure is part of that amalgam, both sponsoring and belonging to it. In *Newark, N. J.*, 1962, we see an ice cream parlor manager looking out from behind his window; the menu stuck to the glass looks like his flimsy breastplate. A step behind him is a boy holding a flag, but it's hard to tell if he is inside or outside. Images of a Fourth of July parade are marooned in the glass. The picture has a gusto, a confrontational force, that is at once brutal and plaintive. That, too, is a distinct American tone. The composition, so apparently happenstance, is canny and self-aware. (Pop bottles are lined up in the window like shooting gallery targets.) Friedlander's streetside images crackle with contrary textures, cheery metallic definitions, but they are disturbed into uncertainty—and thus rescued from the ash-can sentimentality that haunts this kind of straight photography—by the nebulous plying of mirrored surfaces.

In contrast to Minor White's high, trim tonal resolutions and superb hierophantic calm, Friedlander's images are messier, rudely congestive, and always less thought-out; he admits to making a great many exposures then choosing only a very small number of them to print. The exquisite calculations of White's work are necessary and appropriate to the spiritual investigations they externalize; they also function as meditative objects meant to be both exemplary and instructive. Friedlander's work, though crassly secular in its subject matter and execution, bears a more complete sense of the world as materialization of some force of otherness. An image by Minor White is the result of spiritual deliberation; a Friedlander image is expressive of the *process* of deliberation, of moral and social deliberation. If there is a good deal of the social documentarian in Friedlander—as he has continued Atget's project of recording commercial life behind windows, he has also continued Lewis Hine's project of essaying workers in the workplace—there is none of the reformer. Friedlander's first love was jazz. When he was sixteen he heard a recording of Charlie Parker and later commented: "He made me understand that anything is possible." He translated that improvisational spirit into a casual formality of imagery. The jazziness repressed whatever reformist impulse might have tempted him, and it provided working principles: Censor nothing, absorb whatever comes along, keep the process in motion. Jazz is antideterministic, its moods tumbling from gaiety to rasping agony. Friedlander's art developed by following that (non-) directive. If White was a methodical seeker, Friedlander has been a finder.

As a social artist, a student of relations, Friedlander gives play to constellated circumstances. He does not have the colonizing willfulness of formalist photographers like Weston and Paul Strand, whose use of the torn tag ends of physical reality was more an act of transfiguration than one of witness to reality's derangements. When Friedlander takes pictures of mirrors, he finds that familiar photographic conceit in its matrix of use, complete with fake intimacies and unnerving estrangements. Several of his pictures catch the double vision familiar to us when we are driving: the rearview mirror, like an image from a theater of memory, bears its own "present moment" into the moment we actually see before us. We see where we have been only once we have passed it.

Seeker and Finder: Minor White and Lee Friedlander

That kind of dissonance is literally second nature to us. On a primary field of firefighters in white gloves marching in a small town parade, Friedlander floats a rearview-mirror image of a dog and doghouse under a tree surrounded by a piece of perfect lawn. The whole image shocks into relation these bits of reality and enacts the perceptual activity that performs it; its subject is really the way the eye assembles the world.

Even when he is caught by the oddness of a scene, Friedlander drains it of coyness and infuses it with even odder, more disruptive tones. My favorite of this type is a Philadelphia image taken in 1973: a mummers string band costumed as Vikings (they are wearing Valkyrie helmets and have spears like giant hairpins sticking out of their headpieces) is drilling in a schoolyard. The snowy aura of plumes fanning around their heads is rendered even more arctic, though also more tenderly festive, by the dazzling, raw autumn sunlight. Behind them we see the backs of working-class rowhouses with perky TV antennas (more hairpins). And yet the image, for all its charming, goofy details and great light, is sullen and melancholy, perhaps because what we notice most of all is the separateness of the musicians, their weary distractedness or self-absorption, and the dreary routine of rehearsal. The depressive tone does not pull down the image, but it certainly upsets the peppy certainty of those costumes and all that light.

The mummers picture carries on straight photography's tradition of robust matter-of-factness, especially as Friedlander inherits it from Walker Evans and Robert Frank. From Evans he seems to have learned to test the congestive limits of the frame and to find in silver tones a particularly American expression of want amid plenitude. From Frank he learned the dignity of mood and how to isolate from the stream of visual consciousness the critical moment when a relation is exposed. All three artists circle around the one true subject of straight photography: death. The staring innocence of the camera submits in an instant to contingency, the first and forever moment in which an image exists. The solidities and vaporizations of physical reality are audaciously present, while the field of vision is momentarily spared from oblivion. The flatness of the image, the exhaustion of all substance in that flatness, the terminal exhaustion of our dimensioned world, becomes death's purest metaphor. The outrage of the photographic act is to restore completely to consciousness, so painfully and so pleasurably, the existence of someone now dead. We cultivate the outrage by taking snapshots of our lives and the lives of others, because we need it so. Minor White's achievement was remarkable in that he broke down the conventional self-consciousness of mortality usually borne by photographs—a feat only a mystical artist can accomplish. Friedlander's sensibility is both more conventional and more social. His pictures verge sometimes on visual hysteria, and they are occasionally darkened by a sardonic awareness that feels almost like a diabolical coquetry.

When the effects are too calculated, the moods and relations in Friedlander's pictures can be strained to the point of caricature. One of his finest works is the photo-essay *Factory Valleys*, which is set in the landscapes and workplaces of the Ohio rust belt in 1979 and 1980, when America's heavy manufacturing economy was failing fast. Several years later he did a series on computer operators in Boston, the workers whose place in the new high-tech economy corresponds to that once occupied by Ohio welders and drop-forge operators. The word processors at their stations look uniformly zoned out, rigid, pasty, their eyes locked to the little screens. They are cliché; their presentation does nothing to pull us out of our most vulgar assumptions about the blissful affectlessness of high-tech work. The Boston pictures show little of the imaginative sympathy that Friedlander directed at his subjects in *Factory Valleys*. Even though a few of the images of industrial workers derive too predictably from the cliché of numbed laborers in Fritz Lang's *Metropolis*, there is something in the physical nature of their work that charges Friedlander's imagination and makes him find ways of destabilizing familiar forms. The young black woman wiring vacuum-cleaner switches in *Canton, Ohio, 1980* is installed in her scene like a conceit by Paul

Klee, ensnared by the racks of wiring behind her and a power cable looped in front of her like a dopey smile. She is serenely, easefully beautiful, with an aristocratic air that nearly abstracts her from her circumstances. At first look, she is a conventional working-class Black Madonna. But we see also the arduous repetitive mechanical work she is performing, the kind of piecework that entirely defines her station in life, which in time will bring a most unblessèd boredom and pain. There is desire in Friedlander's rendering of the woman, but it is complicated by the circumstances of the place. The image will not allow anyone (or anyone's argument, including my own) to patronize it.

Generally, Friedlander has always needed the vividness and quickened improvisational quality of context. When his images are stripped of intrusive, haphazard circumstance, as are his portraits, family scenes, and nudes, they become ornery and recalcitrant. The space in a photograph by Friedlander is also never a setting or medium of desire, with one exception: the female *Nude, Boston, 1981*, lying with her arms and long hair spread behind her turned head. The body (only the upper torso is visible) floods its space and turns perspective into a strange enactment of craving and voluptuous self-sufficiency. By contrast, even the most stately, aloof interior or male nude by Minor White is, in formal terms, a configuration of desire or spiritual yearning. Friedlander's pictures are appetites, not desires; he wants (like Atget) mainly to acquire and devour, and his images are more infused and determined by need than by purpose. Thus he is quick both to allow into an image accidental, cross-grained feeling-tones and to crease the motif with his own predatory presence. The best of his self-portraits is the one in which he does not really appear, *Canyon de Chelly, Arizona, 1983*, where we see only his full-length shadow cast on tufts of dried grass that radiate like a spikey halo around the shadow's head. The image-maker's colonizing presence becomes immaterial shade over the force of nature. We see at once the arrogant daring, randomness, humility, mortal sense, and inconsequentiality of the encounter.

Friedlander does not seem to respond with much intensity to domestic interiors, and his landscapes often look like industrial sites—with the notable exception of the Japanese landscapes he did in the early 1980s, which have suspenseful painterly effects, like those in Japanese scroll art, and luscious flurried light. He likes candor and vulnerability but seems uninterested in purity or innocence. His images bulge with pokey oddments. He's a poet of the New World afloat on bulky, tacky superfluities, and he has nearly perfect pitch for the varieties of American melancholy. His series on city monuments is especially unsettling: individual soldiers, crouching in bayonet-attack position or standing at port arms, have the same drained, muffled look that's present in their town square surroundings. We recognize the figures as images out of our common imagination; they have neither the air of imperturbable innocence nor the aloof historical heroism that would cut them free from our sense of American theatricality. The Father Duffy statue in *New York, 1974* is embedded in its amassed scene of skyscrapers, street signs, and scaffoldings. In *Saint Albans, Vermont, 1975*, a tree behind the statue of an infantryman grows from his head like antlers or skeletal prehistoric wings. Objects have a soul-life in a culture, and Friedlander exposes in ours a fatigued helplessness borne up by dim but valued memories of glory and bravery. The composition of the monument images holds these elements in a state of tensed self-regard, battening emblems of nationalist feeling to their surroundings as if at any moment they might be blown into chaos—though the dominant mood is one of calm, good order, and self-possession. The effects of the St. Albans image are softened all over by snow.

In other pictures the visual commotion is so turbulent or impacted that the compositional structure hardly has the tensile strength to hold them together. Friedlander likes to admit into his image field the kind of urban pandemonium that we instinctually edit out so that we will not go mad. In an image of New York taken in 1980, a dump truck, cropped front and back in the picture's lower half, is a crude pedestal upon which are heaped tall background buildings that fold back from the picture plane. *They* are the payload, though they are not even rubble yet. The picture is a figure of the manic remaking of our cities, of construction and use and demolition as one sustained activity. In such pictures as this, Friedlander's humor is salted with cynicism and cruelty, and for a moment we can sense his use of the camera not as an analytical or expressive instrument but as a kind of antagonistic, inquisitive Swiftian speech. Atget recorded a new Paris meant to last another millennium (at least). Friedlander represents our anarchic regard for permanent structures, in our material creations as well as our social organizations, even when our better instincts tell us to preserve or conserve at all costs. His images seldom have the high resolution of inalterability, of the perfect realization of a supreme instant. In fact, they look as if they could be repaired, fixed up, *worked* up. Not improved, but maybe dismantled, revised, urban-renewed. In his pictures, even stone and brick, in their American moment, look vitreous and glazed, and windowglass looks like silver-tinted, thinned-out stone.

Ten Takes

Henri Matisse

One of Matisse's many serene but disruptive images is the modest *Large Interior, Nice,* from 1918. The view into the room is so steeply pitched that we are looking down at the top of a chair. Deeper in the picture, on the other side of the room, a woman sits on a chair on a terrace, the sea and sky looming behind her. At first the painting looks like a decorative exercise in colorist dynamics. But once we are "inside" the picture, which is to say once we are drawn into the recognitions of space that the image enacts, Matisse shifts the axis so that the overhead view or entry tilts to become a straight-ahead view. He changes the space so that we feel we are moving within the scene the moment we are made to look down upon it. There are no histrionics in the gesture. The strange career of the eye through the image is conducted with the same foxy ease that Matisse exercised in so many of his decorative interiors. Breton once said that art should be convulsive, and Matisse's art certainly has that quality, though it is never theatrical. Convulsiveness is never the controlling issue or effect; it is instead a feeling-tone kneaded into the work of interrogating space and color, and of making the painting surface answerable to complex sensations. For a cool, steady worker like Matisse, tumult is played out as troubled normalcies. I kept circling back to that Nice painting during my visits to the big 1992 Matisse retrospective at the Museum of Modern Art, and the more familiar it became, the more unsettling were its effects. Even more unsettling was the simian head on the middle figure in *Three Bathers with a Turtle.* Matisse took this classical motif, deploying his three tall loose figures with placidly distributed energies of color and line, then literally capped it with the most savage and roughly rendered head in his entire work, almost as if he meant to convulse the illusion of evolutionary stability the rest of the image creates. Matisse practiced a rich hedonistic style; his pictures give immediate intoxicating physical pleasure. But his work is also the embodiment of a fairly constant state of bad nerves. The fragmented or re-dimensioned spaces, the fauvist jangle, the stressed-out figure drawing, the rent veils and separated color fields, the delirium of decoration in his interiors, the curtailed ecstasies in his images of dancers and musicians—they become, especially in a massive retrospective exhibition, a processional extravaganza of just barely muffled discontents. Matisse was, on the ample evidence of the recent show, the most anxious and least happy of voluptuaries. Any image of whole and entire delight was bound to break down in his hands. His was a cool, workable melancholy. He could not express desire without also expressing, with equal intensity, his uncertainty about the realization of desire.

Richard Diebenkorn

In the early work of the 1940s, under the influence of Clyfford Still and Rothko, Diebenkorn often worked up corrosive, abraded surfaces in his paintings; the passion of form-finding was registered in the textures of the pigment, and yet the passion looked studied and exact. With his celebrated turn to figurative painting in 1955, his palette became more reserved and demure, his attack more structural than atmospheric. His figures do not occupy space so much as they are fused to it; light seems to adhere to flesh, not to fall upon it. The objects in the genre scenes— coffee cups, studio sink, cigarettes, chairs, tables, windows—have a cultivated ordinariness, the numinous quietude of household gods. Compared to the meaty paint and druidic figuration of his colleague David Park, Diebenkorn's paintings look becalmed and depersonalized, certainly less raucous and extreme. What makes the work from that figurative period so compelling, in fact, is its withheld energies, a vaguely restless decorousness that carried over into the abstract painting Diebenkorn returned to in the late 1960s. The Ocean Park series he commenced when he moved to Santa Monica in 1967 and continued to produce through the 1970s is at once analytical and sensuously atmospheric. He somehow found a way of blending formal deliberation with extravagant moodiness. In the bigger Ocean Park canvases, he let pentimenti seep through the "finish" of the paintings. The cutaway views of his revisions, corrections, remakings, were part of the symphonic effects created by the completed work. Each picture was a kind of record of analytical changes of heart. The veils of pigment, the often redrawn or painted-over frames and bars and lattices that edge the paintings, the color washes and scrupulously reworked palimpsests of sketchwork, all helped to make these paintings testaments of a lush tentativeness. Every canvas was a fossilized process of its own evolution. Two of the precedents for this activity were Matisse, with his veiled effects and unfinished passages, and Giacometti, whose work was always an agony of inadequacy. Diebenkorn methodically took over the problem and the passion but expressed them both as cool, Californian restlessness that was neither convulsive nor destructive. Close up, the Ocean Park paintings teem with little actions, the inexact gravities of pigment, the twitchy or elegant wrist movements in the drawing, the pressurizing of color fields by those knifey margins, the mysterious outlining that in one stroke goes from hard to wooly, lightly braided colors set next to dense, impacted areas, blistered effects created in thinned pigment, seething white-on-white passages—the procession of effects from painting to painting is stately, imperturbable, restive in a cunning way, and always acting out an interrogation of the sensations created by painted forms on a flat surface. Diebenkorn's passion was of a steady, even kind. We seldom feel the presence of a disordering or disruptive temperament. He often spent a very long time working up certain paint-

Ten Takes

ings, poking and pushing until the painting became, as he liked to say, "fixed," achieved, realized as if by its own formal volition. Sometimes a picture completed itself when the perfect and just mistake finally happened, when compartmentalized registers of color leaked or bled into adjoining cells, or when overpainting—blues on greens, grays over yellows, ochres over blues—destabilized a structure and caused it to fall into a new and satisfying compound. That was when the painting, disheveled into good structure, could (like a piece of poetry) be *stopped*.

Edouard Vuillard

In his dense, crabbed interiors of French bourgeois households, Vuillard paints the sluggish physical solidity of things. Tabletops, mantels, antimacassars, mirrors, drapes, pianos and pitchers and silverware, have a heft and immediacy weighted down by endearing familiarity. They possess the hugginess and soulfulness of household objects we might remember from our childhood homes, our imagination loading remembrance with its own moody charge. (The human figures in the paintings have the same inescapable proximity.) With this familiarity comes also a ponderous and vexatious domesticity, the too familiar textures and volumes that can suffocate and oppress us, in memory if not in fact, the encumbrances that would turn selfhood into nothing but residues of family and home-place. A bedstead or armchair becomes so soggy with associations of the past that it can have no new life in the present, no freshness in consciousness. The objects and figures in Vuillard's interiors, especially the great ones of the 1890s, seem conspirators in the routine of a life too well known. In the way he builds up and amasses paint, we can feel the *effort* of imaginative recovery. If it is an expression of love, it is love exercised as a difficult, glacial kind of prayer, tedious but hopeful. Some of the 1890s paintings have atmospheres so blistery and portentous that we feel the bourgeois codes of those households have become a moral rigor worked into the crusty tonalities of the pigment and the intensely contractile space. Most of us carry through life conflicted feelings about the dear and dreadful household implements and decorations of our childhood homes. Vuillard is the master painter of those conflicted states, though there is no turbulence in the paintings. He draws us in because the familiarity of those sofas, those tablecloths, those warm dense bodies of women, all invite us into a world of comforting safety, but the invitation turns clammy, or creepy, with all the minutely amassed memento mori of a present not yet dead. In Vuillard's representation of the things of our ordinary lives, all time is posthumous.

Fairfield Porter

For Porter, Vuillard's most eloquent American champion, domestic life was enacted as open-air adventures. He painted interiors as if they were a casual American antimatter to the cobbled, stifling intimacies of Vuillard. He made interiors such assemblages of diaphanous light that we feel we are always outdoors. Household objects such as tables, chairs, vases, children's toys, and bric-a-brac have a buoyant improvisational presence. Unlike the world of things in Vuillard's universe, where matter seems fateful and laden with destinies, Porter's material world looks as if it could go up in smoke (or dissipate into pure shapeless light) at any moment. The figures who occupy those household spaces are not stolid inhabitants or severe stewards of circumstance, they are brilliant visitors, migratory presences that alight on a scene, smile (or not), stare distractedly into nowhere, then disappear. They are not welded into their material surround. Porter learned a great deal from Vuillard, but the paintings he made in the last ten years of his life, from 1965 to 1975, show a free handling and ventilated mood that are entirely his own. The joy in his love for domestic settings is not abridged by severities; the interiors bear no darkened residue of pastness as an oppression in consciousness. This is not simply American freshness (not only that, anyway); it is a particular regard for matter and the way it creates or houses space. (The Fairfield Porter who wrote canny, tart, and funny art criticism most of his life would remind us that the only matter that counts is the matter of pigment.) Porter's interiors do not close down and make us hostage to their moods, as Vuillard's often do. His pictures usually look casual and loose, especially those which include family members or his poet friends John Ashbery and James Schuyler, but the mercurial effects are created by means of a rigorous structure. In the 1968 *Self-Portrait*, the painter looms in the foreground, and as the depth of field opens behind him, the shape of space and the objects it contains—the stove, a water bottle on the floor, a chair, pictures on the walls, a window, a house in yellow light beyond the window, a skylight, tree limbs above the skylight—occur to the eye with the casual exactitude and purposefulness with which the words of a poem fall upon the ear.

Camille Pissarro

Pissarro said it was not contour that mattered but interior color and value, and his painting owes its ardent intensities to those qualities. In *Pont Boieldieu, Rouen: Sunset 1886*, the light amassed under the bridge looks like a cobbled supporting wall, but it is a structure without an outline—it's at once a vacancy and a momentous substance, a vapor and a sustaining consistency. Pissarro achieves vivid expansive and contractile effects entirely through his use of color, especially in his paintings of street scenes, and he creates a sense of scale by building up relations of color and value. What he gives up is the articulate energy of contour, its elasticity and testiness. He was, by all reports, a helpful and attentive teacher. Two of his students, Cézanne and Matisse, building on his instruction and example, developed ways of making pictures in which part of the drama was the challenged relations between color and contour, substance and margin. These relations were so pleasurably unstable that in time both Matisse and Cézanne made pieces of art in which completion and unfinishedness were folded together as one purpose. In Cézanne's late landscapes, phantasmal contours are fixed by patches of unpainted canvas; the blankness of the painting's surface became part of the drama of values. Matisse's most powerful expressions of embodiment are his large simple outlines of dancers and fauns and nudes. Flooding the embodiment of color against the energy of outline, these pictures have a physical effect on me that I've never felt looking at Pissarro's work. I feel such a charge from them (and from works of their kind) that I step back, clearing a space for their aura. It's politically suspect, and probably a bit primitive, to acknowledge and value aura. That cleared space, the energy field, has its origins in ancient religions, but its modern and most familiar expression is Coleridge's figure of possession in "Kubla Khan":

> Weave a circle round him thrice,
> And close your eyes with holy dread,
> For he on honey-dew hath fed,
> And drunk the milk of Paradise.

Madness, magic, and good pharmaceuticals. But aura requires embodiment first, and embodiment in painting is a matter of putting shapeful colors on a surface, as poetry is a matter of putting words in a certain order, even though the force stirred up by those colors or words may be disorderly or disordering.

Marsden Hartley

Again, that physical force that certain paintings throw out: two works by Hartley exert it so exactly that they make me want to answer it with action. I should do a jig in their presence, or roll around on the floor, or hoot back from a safe distance. *Crow with Ribbons* in the National Gallery displays a dead crow on a white beribboned sheet. The brilliant contrast of black on white intensifies the weight of the crow, the heavy flesh and feathers, a moral heft that is a kind of pictorial reprisal for all the traditional disgusting associations of crows and carrion, the ballads that sing of anxious crows picking the eyes of a poor slain knight who has no one to grieve for him. Hartley's crow, denatured for art, has a sensual glamor and hungry calm. As still life, *natura morta*, it haunts us because Hartley paints the motif with a cozy mischievous mirth indistinguishable from profound love of matter. In *Wild Roses*, hanging above the mantel in a room in the Phillips Collection, the crisply drawn flowers are painted with a high-key, mineral feverishness. In their voluptuous physical repose—Hartley paints them as if they were the Venus of flowers—they seem self-aware of inflicting their heavy beauty on our tired familiar ideas of beauty. Both of these paintings enact a recognition of the grand fiction of atomic consistency, the held-togetherness of particles that element physical reality. Surely this is a compactness, a compact, that cannot come undone. Surely matter binds and holds and stays.

Susan Rothenberg

In the 1970s, critics hopeful of a breakthrough in representational painting rallied to Rothenberg's work. Her robust images of horses had no trickery in them. They issued from a noble, recognizable tradition of figure drawing but also built on certain advances made by abstract painting in the 1950s and 1960s. Representational and carefully modeled, they yet had no illusionist depth and showed the kind of "in progress" surfaces we associate with de Kooning. The paintings also invoked prehistoric cave images. Rothenberg's horses have a mythic suggestiveness, a story-ness, a sense of being an image residue of what once was fact. In their self-awareness as images, they remind me of certain lines from Edwin Muir's poem "The Horses," in which farmers who long ago replaced horses with tractors, now useless after a devastating nuclear war, are visited by horses running loose: "We saw the heads / Like a wild wave charging and were afraid." For all their strangeness in life, the horses are familiar as representations, "As fabulous steeds set on an ancient shield / Or illustrations in a book of knights." Rothenberg's images are at once an expression of embodiment and animal nature and also a self-consciously evolved pictorial *idea* of horses. Often laid on or webbed into a grid or cross pattern (like the skeletal geometries in Leonardo's drawings), the images are built up in shadowy or lightly impastoed paints. They are cast as remembrances, not only as an animal remembered but as an image remembered, something recovered for an image archive, designated "HORSE." Done in acrylics, Rothenberg's horse paintings achieved smoky but dense effects, aura and embodiment. In the 1980s, as she explored other subjects, some of that early passion drained away or faded. She became more caught up in the local energies of painting. (She was also changing from acrylics to oils.) The brushwork gets choppier, more curt and anxiety-ridden. Though much of her work in that period was, by Rothenberg's own admission, in homage to Mondrian, to the purity and clarity of formal decisiveness, the paintings often have the scarifying, snaggletooth action of Giacometti. In one painting she pictures herself dancing with Mondrian (who, it is said, always preferred to dance alone) but the dance takes place under a Giacometti rainstorm of paint in a dancehall that looks decorated by de Kooning. Maybe the liability for an artist original in her early work (and so timely and appropriate to certain critical needs and expectations) is that she may have to postpone the work of negotiating her crucial influences and derivations. What painter (or poet) can glide through such a process? Testimonials, conflicts, false or provisional resolutions, denunciations, homages, tweakings, and detonations— the time to power through these troubles is when one is younger. It's

Ten Takes

cautionary to witness a gifted artist like Rothenberg struggling candidly and arduously with certain influences in her late forties, after having struck so solidly and originally nearly twenty years ago.

Edvard Munch

Although the pictures most familiar to us are the chilly nocturnes and the pinched, staring or wailing figures he painted in the 1890s, Munch produced a great many paintings from 1919 until his death in 1944. Many of them treat sexual relations, especially the relations between artist and model. Munch painted the model as the embodiment of his own perplexed desire, and into the space separating model and artist he poured aggrieved fury and tense resentment. During that later period, he produced numerous versions of the Eden myth. In *Man and Woman in the Garden I*, the aging, angular figure of the artist appears in correct bourgeois attire—bowler hat, buttoned up jacket, closed collar. He looks at a woman dressed in a loose short-sleeved white dress. Flowers and fruit fill the air around and between them, choking the surface of the painting like water hyacinths. The succulent productions of nature float wanton and numerous in the space of the painting. In this modern Garden, the fruit and flowers are not so much a festive bounty as a wilderness of violently proliferating confusion. This Garden of sexual anticipation is a place of plenitude and oblivion. The artist Adam, locked up in his clothes, is all watchful, predatory normalcy. The social isolation of earlier works like *The Scream* and *The Voice* becomes in the later work a menacing anxiety of fused or lost identities. The emotional key is usually voracity, however disguised it may be in bourgeois rituals or the conventions of atelier genre painting. Much has been written about the misogyny and dread in Munch's later work. The 1916 *Vampire* is the locus classicus. A woman bends over the nape of a man's neck, her red hair streaming down and around them both like powerful hands holding them in their passion. She is sucking his blood, and the image therefore expresses (the argument goes) Munch's fear and chastisement of a woman's passion, that it will suck away his life-blood, which for an artist means sucking blood from the work. But the male figure has his head pressed into the woman's lap, and it is not reposing there, it is sucking. The vampire of the title is the one creature the two of them compose. With the loose handling which in his later work becomes so unsettling, because the looseness somehow tightens the emotional range and makes sexual feeling seem a neurotic paralysis, Munch imbues the reciprocal vampirism, that blood-relatedness, with a scary tenderness. The image could have been titled *The Kiss*. The partners fuse into one flooding body of passion. Nothing is stilled or fixed or held back. Each figure drains away into the other. It is the pure undifferentiated lostness of ecstasy, of coming. That flooding cannot be remembered, it can only be reimagined—we reinvent to remember.

Clyfford Still

Still's grandest works for me are like those of a tensed-up northern Protestant tempted by the operatic agonies of warm southern Catholicism. The large canvases of the 1960s, with their craggy color fields ripped by toothy, high-contrast wedges, certainly don't seem cool or rationalist or severe. I feel I'm in the presence of a tormented, heroic enterprise, one intent on forcing abstractionist scale to yield grace notes and nuance. And yet the same surfaces that enact the enterprise are dry, dry, dry, and *chilly*, even when Still is using hot yellows and lavic reds. Even in the early work of the late 1940s and early 1950s, more condensed but in many ways more turbulent than the large format work that would follow, he was becoming the driest, least juicy painter among those abstractionists who wanted the canvas to record the immediacy of formal feeling, formal discovery. There's a lot of conflict worked into the surfaces of the 1960s work, the fire-lick forms that seem like emulsions melting from within the image. They are images of Puritan intimacy and severity scaled to express broad extravagant moral feeling. Rothko, who learned much from Still's example in the 1940s when they were in California together, risks a shameless Coriolanian moodiness in his large glowing pictures. Still's images, by contrast, look *stricken.* Arterial reds and browns, even when the paint is laid on in palette-knife loads, are desiccated. The blacks and purples look carbonized, powdery, not pitchy or moist. The estuarial shapes seamed into the larger color masses look fossilized, a record of their own ambitious intent. I feel in all of Still's work a fastidious, quarrelsome temperament giving shape to its rigorous deliberations. In its austere way, it's defiantly anti-Californian. Still seems to dare us to relax in the presence of these images. There is not a trace of fake religious icon-mongering in his canvases, but there is much concentration of religious feeling.

Francis Bacon

In the last ten years of his life, Bacon handled paint more loosely and gesturally than ever before, but the effects were anything but casual. In the big portraits and multipanel works, the human body becomes even more voluminous and massive. (The genius remembered in these paintings is the youthful, stolid Masaccio, not the aged, racy Titian.) The violence is not mellowed, it's intensified. Where in earlier Bacon paintings the cranium or face is blurred by a swipe of a sponge or rag, in his late works the head is clipped or effaced into a mess of forms. In a 1985 self-portrait blood sprays from the head where the side has been sheared away. Bacon always felt some kind of nervous rage at the head, because it is the seat of deliberation, and he attacked it with a peculiarly focused intensity in his last years, as if to make the body a ganglion of flesh, all nerves and instinct. In many of the paintings, shadows droop at the feet of the figures or dribble across thresholds or sills like useless rags dragged around by the flesh. Bacon handles shadow with vague indifference, as if it were a smudged replica of life. Anything that is not embodied is mere shade, pale underworld wraiths unworthy of the vivacities and violent dynamisms of flesh. The monolithic backgrounds—ochres, aquamarines, mudstone grays, and yellows—have a palpable solidity and density and yet do not menace or threaten to absorb the figures exposed there. The body occupies its space, its ground of color, with stunning sexual force. We can sense the quickening of sexual appetite in the coiled, wormy, muscle-rind bodies resisting the consistencies and evened-out monochromes of those brilliant grounds. For Bacon, nature's compass was the human body in a room: on a bed alone or wrestling or coupling with another, on the toilet, at a washbasin, in a chair or doorway, bloodied or glisteningly pristine, hair and skin hackles plastered sleek or bristling like pine needles. It's a creepy cliché by now, but no less true for that: the body represented in oil paint on a flat surface was, for Bacon, the completest visual answer to the intensities of embodiment.

· **III** ·

Out of Notebooks

WHAT IS HARDEST TO CONFESS IS NOT WHAT IS CRIMINAL,
BUT WHAT IS RIDICULOUS AND SHAMEFUL.

Rousseau

I write poetry to seek not serene wisdom but a state of nerves that's deliberative and self-aware, an intensity of the moral moment. I'm put off, in my own work and in the work of others, by intellectual decoration. I believe temperament is critical in determining the rhythms and textures of a poet's language. By temperament choleric and melancholic, I expect my work to be dyed with these colors. Lacking patience and tranquil expansiveness, I'm drawn to poets who create capacious symphonic effects, to Wordsworth in particular. Especially the Wordsworth of "The Ruined Cottage" and the first version of *The Prelude*, where the life of consciousness and moral consequence opens in a broad physical context. Wordsworth couldn't achieve what his sometime friend Coleridge achieved. He could not turn rudeness or clatter or splinteriness or fragmentariness into a virtue, into formal compositional elements. Wordsworth's longer poems have a rich and heavy hanging scenery, while Coleridge's poems, even "Christabel" and the "Rime," seem racy sketches. Diderot says somewhere that sketches represent a fevered love and energy on the artist's part "with no admixture of the affected elaboration introduced by thought: through the sketch the artist's very soul is poured forth on the canvas."

· · ·

Nearly all the checkout clerks at my local supermarket speak Spanish and English. Sometimes a clerk chatting with the customer ahead of me will glance back at me then switch from English to Spanish. I look at the women and men, mostly working people in manual or secretarial jobs, many of them with kids, and in the kids I see our future poets, from a culture that contains and protects them in the envelope of its own language and customs, though there's violence, too, and all sorts of discontent and trouble. I think some of these children will write poetry in an English saturated with the manners and feeling tones of their native language and maybe cauled by a memory of a distant place. It will be pure mongrel American. Their poetry will remember the work of today's Latino poets; with an arrogance and impatience that poets have to exercise, they may respect their predecessors for clearing a way but criticize them for relying too much on local color, cultural anecdotalism, and bully politics. At home in their languages, they drag along behind their parents' shopping carts in the big bland Lucky's supermarket in this bland suburban setting. Bland except for the dazzling storefront display one block down from Lucky's, the one that reminds me so piercingly of the festive colors of open air markets in Italian cities. "El Mercadito Latino," its bins overflowing with cobbled textures of limes, avocados, oranges, bananas, lemons, and apples. The poets are there, buying plantains and tomatillos with their mothers. When the clerk finishes talking with the mothers in Spanish, she looks at me and asks: "Is that all for today?"

* * *

Yesterday I was walking down Via San Vitale in Bologna, having just come from Via San Leonardo, the working-class quarter where the colors of the housefronts wane through hues of red and yellow and orange, a synoptic seasonality on the plaster, while along the portico people walked briskly, shopped at the unmarked produce stand that just last week was a garage, or swept the pavements. But I ended up on Via San Vitale, one of the main streets that spoke toward the center of town where the two towers stand. Asinelli, tall and complete despite the earthquakes that rattled it in earlier times. And Garisenda, Dante's tower, which in his poem gives scale and vertiginous pitch to the figure of the giant Antaeus, leaning over the Pilgrim on hell's floor. Before coming to the towers, I passed my favorite palazzo, il *Fantuzzi*, called *Il palazzo degli elefanti* because of the large ornamental carvings of elephants on the facade, a funny and extravagantly oriental decoration on these medieval streets. The years have eroded the stonework; the years and cars and carbon monoxide. The elephants' high relief has been planed nearly flat, bleared—they look like yesterday's sand castles. The sunlight, slanting down through the portico pillars, rules the shadows into even parts. The sun dials across the pavements. Smoke, fumes, odors of busses, cigarettes, coffee machines, perfumes and colognes, cheese and salami, and vehicles of all sorts hovering down the narrow street. A lady pedals by on an old bicycle that seems made of wrought iron, she is wearing a mink coat and kid gloves, I can see the beautiful balled shape of knucklebones and wrist. I said to myself, This is my place. This is not my place. I've always been here, and never really so, because I always feel like a visitor wherever I am. While walking down Via San Vitale I was where I am, in Redwood City, California, where there are no redwoods, where there are few tall trees of any kind. Redwood City is famous for having the most moderate weather west of the Rockies; the town's official motto used to be "Climate Best, by Government Test." The elephants look down on me as I say it, shedding their outlines.

⋄ ⋄ ⋄

Intellectual nostalgia, I thought, rereading Camus. Some feebleness in the need to recover (if it's even possible) the austerity and force of his books that I felt twenty-five years ago:

Out of Notebooks

To understand is, above all, to unify. The mind's deepest desire, even in its most elaborate operations, parallels man's unconscious feeling in the face of his universe: it is an insistence upon familiarity, an appetite for clarity . . . . That nostalgia for unity, that appetite for the absolute illustrates the essential impulse of the human drama.

Form in poetry is an expression of that nostalgia, but the absolute is not what I want. I want the appetite, the plasticity of that. It's not the wish for perfection. (Perfection is charming but uninteresting.) Poetry's formal energies are appetitive because they insist, often in a disorderly way, on the acquisition of all the particulars of experience, of an impossible sum and constellation of instances. The forms of poetry may be a judicious processional or a dizzy dance, but they are always a masque enacting nostalgia for the absolute. The constant incompleteness and incompletability of that activity, of the exercise of that appetite, is one story a poet may tell. Or, I should say, the forms of poetry tell or narrate *us*.

*   *   *

A photo by Roman Vishniac of Jews in the Warsaw Ghetto. Falling snow, men standing outdoors dressed in shabby ill-fitting overcoats, shoes that are too large (the toes curl as if recoiling from the cold ground), long white and dark beards set off against the black buildings and bright snow. The mothy snow falls and stops, suspended leafily in the air of the picture, soft but obliterating, because there seem to be too many snowflakes falling, with no sign of warmth or shelter anywhere. It's an image of exposure and reduction. Not diminution, for the figures look dominant and occupy so much space, thanks to those huge coats. The enclosures, the buildings, awnings, shawls, shoes, even the snow cowling the entire scene—every bit is expressive of exposure. The figures don't exist in or with the elements, they suffer them. Heavily wrapped as they are, they are bare fork'd creatures.

. . .

Paradise is where objects have a hard bright singleness not numbed or clouded by habit, by what Baudelaire calls "the heavy darkness of communal and day-to-day existence." The more habituated we become, while objects proliferate so riotously in our culture, the harder it is to keep the sensors alive and sharp, to preserve our Eden sense. Maybe we are so flooded by objects of habit that we live in a nearly constant state of distraction from the shining particulars of existence that strike us on every page of Homer, and we tend to seek meanings, privileged meanings, in whatever is idiosyncratic or strange. We insist more and more on certain moments, picked from the bin of identical parts, as unique, freighted with meaning or consequence, the privilege of details noticed, notions entertained. The poet in a secular time still nostalgic for the absolute (but unable or unwilling to engage that discipline) will confer on the entirely subjective moment the singular brilliance of Paradise. Our poetry insists on this. We live with a sense of bereavement, and of it we make a poetry that knows but is reluctant to admit that the world outside consciousness is made up simply of this, that, and the other thing. If Eden is what we want it to be, it is not Eden.

. . .

What's wrong with our poetry is that it's worried about being right. Heartthrob platitudes, huggy anecdotalism, outraged stridencies over injustice in countries to which the poet migrates in search of worthy subjects, scrupulous self-censorship in the interest of preserving morally pristine responses to the facts of experience, lines that confuse form with metrical or sentimental purity, agonies endured (or sworn to) entirely for the "appropriate dramatic fullness" of a poem, classroom vocabularies that determine the formal emotional deliberations in the writing of poetry, valiant eloquence in defense of poetry—"our" poetry—against philistines who ask who killed poetry . . . . Poetry needs to be defended most against those who most righteously defend it and who identify the life of poetry with the life of a career. Does it matter? Poetry, which exists in all of its words but which does not need only words for its existence, has nothing to fear from even its most illustrious and impassioned agents, even from its most valiant apologists, who know in their hearts that they ennoble poetry by choosing to speak of it. Poetry has nothing to fear from advocates of any new formalism for whom formal mysteries exist as occasions for polemical opportunism, for ever more gleaming correctnesses. The new decorum declares that no argument, no line or phrase of song or great speech, disturb the pieties of the interested party. Why do so many pant for occasions that will allow them to exhibit grand sorrowing, or religious exaltation, or Aristotelian balance and measure? Those who feel that poetry belongs to them, and that American poetry is their share of cultural real estate, may smell of success in the world and shine with the friction of praise rubbed on their surfaces by so many hands. Poetry belongs to them, and that is part of the scheme of rectitude and valor, and so may they never realize that they do not belong to poetry. Then it will be sure of going on, needless, unannounced, unprotected, unheard of.

. . .

The first early winter rain, after three years of drought, comes just before dawn. I thought I heard the falling drops inside my head, felt them somehow even before I heard them, little sleep drumrolls, then came the tangy charred odor that finally woke me.

Rain now off and on for two days. Too soon, they say. (After drought years!) Vintners worry about the harvest. The grapes, especially the delicate whites, need a long dry season. And yet the rain feels restorative, an indifferent pounding plenitude.

. . .

A well-behaved poetry, self-assured and anxious not to displease, makes politeness into a suave arrogance. Good manners thus become a way of coercing readers into admiration. Coerced, they think they are being charmed. This is our own Alexandrianism, maybe appropriate to the end of our century, but it's politically dangerous.

. . .

Coleridge, mad dog of discriminations and divisiveness—"Sea, hill, and wood, / This populous village! Sea, and hill, and wood"—*suffered* the differences among things. He suffered most the abyss separating nature from consciousness. Wordsworth is the surveyor of things come together in mutual blessing. He views consciousness, he does not suffer it. Words-worth is quick to admit any stranger to his banquet. Coleridge must first question any stranger as to his origins and destination and means of travel. Then he goes back to the kitchen to revise the evening's menu.

. . .

In one of his essays Eliade says that poets try to remake the world, to see it as if neither time nor history exists, and that this attitude is much like that of the "primitive," of the person in traditional society. We don't live in a traditional society. Most poets coming out of the European tradition, certainly those in North America, write out of the ruins or remnants or inchoate beginnings of different traditions, dozens of traditions, religious, mythological, familial, and political. I know that a poet seeks and, when fortunate, succeeds in seeing (to borrow Eliade's

Out of Notebooks

phrase) *in illo tempore*, in the First Time, the Early Time, in or near Paradise, the word which means walled garden. But poets write of and with the body, which is pure contingency, time, and an image of history. I may desire to remake or re-see the world in its First Time, as it was in the beginning, but I know in that moment of desire that it is a picture of impossibility, that I write out of the contingency of body, hour, event. If the "pure" or "primitive" poet seeks to remake the world, he or she does so in the shadow of Nimrod, master builder of the Tower of Babel.

. . .

A tradition in Abruzzo used to be to take a newborn infant after it has been washed and wrapped, and set it down on the earth so that it touches its first mother and its soul is "grounded." I like to believe my father was thus grounded, though I have no proof that he was. Born here instead of "over there," I should have been made to touch the ground. It might have helped me mineralize the vapors of imagination.

. . .

In *The Varieties of Religious Experience*, William James says that the life of religion consists of the belief "that there is an unseen order, and that our supreme good lies in harmoniously adjusting ourselves thereto." Much poetry, however, comes from the process of failing to so adjust, or of the torment and struggle to adjust, the dissonance and raucousness of the work of it. I believe a poet's work is to tell the struggle, to attempt to reveal the order or our dream of it. Poetry that convincingly and freshly declares knowledge of that harmony or makes sweet music of that agreement is very rare. Traherne and Vaughan do it. Such poetry may be a little superfluous, for who needs to have represented what has been so supremely experienced? To satisfy religious desire, Hopkins turned language itself into a kind of gigantomachy.

*　　*　　*

I was attracted to church decoration when I was young not only because
my house was austere and drab, but because church statuary, instruments,
stained glass, and wall reliefs thrilled me physically. The narratives and
sacred anecdotes represented in glass, or in the Stations of the Cross that
marked a Way up and down the church aisles, melted to a plain, satisfy-
ing sensuousness of forms. The marble reliefs of the Stations were sexy.
The pumiced curves of bicep and buttock, the turned foot or muscled
thigh or rippling brow were stunning emergencies of flesh. I often imag-
ined reaching my hand out to stroke the tense forearm of a centurion or
of one of the women crowding around Christ as he climbs to Golgotha.
They reminded me of the pale muscular flesh of my parents and relatives,
which I was allowed to see uncovered only during brief vacations at the
Jersey shore in summers. The stained glass images were very different, not
at all familial or fleshly. They gleamed only by virtue of light originating
outside, drenched with a holiness that seemed almost alien to the church
itself. More than those voluptuous wall carvings, the figures of disciples
and saints in the stained glass, the images of lamb, bull, eagle, and dove,
not only begged for a response but dictated the kind of response. They
predetermined desire and drained it of its charge, its fever. The remote-
ness of the Stations, their material self-containment, made desire looser
and wilder, more fanciful even. My feelings could play in the space
between the stone and my self. During Good Friday ceremony, a large
crucifix was set down by the altar rail—I remember the Christ being about
my size, I was ten years old—and like the other devotees I approached the
image on my knees and kissed its feet. In that moment all my feelings for
the anxiety, the suffering and death, the promise of resurrection and
restoration of a life elsewhere—those feelings froze in me, I was unwilling
to surrender them to an image of Christ that was so singular, grabbily real-
istic, and literal. The small distance of desire between me and the images
of the Stations was crucial to my belief. I needed room to work.

Out of Notebooks

. . .

A pure American tone? The yellow of the kitchen-stool vinyl on which James Stewart climbs to test his acrophobia in *Vertigo*. It's the yellow of postwar American prosperity that Richard Nixon bragged about to Nikita Khrushchev. Aggressive cheer, boastful self-confidence, strident belief in work and getting ahead: *Vertigo*'s yellow is blazon for these values. The same values that were toyed with, mocked, and exploited to great commercial success by certain Pop artists of the 1960s, who took over the dandy yellow that gleams like chrome but looks saturated with creamy yellow papaya pulp. Or the coppery red wall coverings in Ernie's, where Stewart first sees the woman he will lose twice. That red, too, became a flashy Pop favorite, and the red of the Coke sign that pops up somewhere in the movie. The colors are not tantalizing, but annunciatory. They don't stir desire, they announce desire's fulfillment, in the signs of material well-being. It's a joy that wants no suggestion of danger or peril around to disturb its perfections, but in the story there is menace and uncertain desire and loss. Having lost the woman he loved, Stewart finds another and recreates her in that lost perfect image, only to discover that she is the original one after all. Discovering that, he loses her a second time.

. . .

In the house where I grew up, I used to wake before anyone else so that I'd have the early morning hours to read books before going to school. Reading was a blissful, auroral time; school was dutiful and hollow. I sat in our one parlor chair, an old worn mohair that shone under the light of my lamp. Outside, cars revved up, men got a 5:30 start to work, the milkman came by in his truck. In the strange swoon of reading, a book cocked in my lap—Freddy the Pig stories, King Arthur adventures, *A Tale of Two Cities*—I watched the textures and bulk of objects change, their intensities dimming or brightening as if reality's temperature was going up and down. The stirring of the words induced it. The wallpaper, the sofa, the Wildwood boardwalk souvenirs like the scallop glass ashtray holding bright nuggets of saltwater taffy, the narrow knick-knack shelves displaying ceramic figurines of Alpine shepherds and milkmaids, the devotional statuettes of St. Jude and the Infant of Prague, all quivered like phantasmagoria. They were at once terribly weighty and dreamily immaterial. That fever of seeing was the infection of the words I was reading. If I could see the objects now, that boy-girl monarch of the world, or the black-and-white snapshots of aunts and uncles looking out at me from their backgrounds, the concrete backyards strung with clothesline, the stolid brick fronts of rowhouses, the wooly air of boardwalks, I know they would look shabby, maybe pathetic, maybe genteel. But only until imagination's fever brings them back, the spirit of memory re-seeing them *toward words*, burning again. What was that plaster figurine of the happy Dutch boy happily shouldering his milkpail yoke? My father went to work while I sat there reading, to paint hospital walls and furniture with Dutch boy paints. By the door, the milkman left a fresh bottle.

◦ ◦ ◦

We brood so much on childhood and adolescence because we know how formative and determinant they were. We make of their events and personalities an allegory which, if fully witnessed and understood, will instruct us (we trust) about how we are still being formed and shaped by experience now. If indeed we believe that adulthood is process, a time of continued spiritual motion and progress, and not a tyranny of norms, habits, and childhood legends. By inquiring *anything* of our early life we ask to be allowed to go on being in process of becoming. Reflection and recollection thus become one act of prayer.

◦ ◦ ◦

Out of Notebooks

When I was in my twenties I studied Yeats's prose—the essays and *Auto-biographies*, not *A Vision*—nearly as much as his poetry. It gave me a sense of the way poetry issues from workaday intellectual activity. In college, it seemed that all the poets I read wrote prose of one kind or another. Milton, Dryden, Keats, Shelley, Crane, Eliot, Pound, Williams. I must have been persuaded that when poets were not writing poetry they were writing something else (or translating). Yeats's power was his ability to keep the poetry and prose in excited balance, as Keats did with his letters. Keats was exemplary because he conducted his education in public, both in the processional developments in the poems and in the letters. Eliot seemed, for all his apparent authority, evasive in a priestly way. Lawrence was fearless, obnoxious, a gusher, exciting because uncontainable. Although Tate, Ransom, Schwartz, Lowell, and Berry-man were all college teachers, I had no notion that a poet's place was in a creative writing program and that classroom pontification would soon become the common substitute for a poet's prose practice, and that the workshop would become the public.

.   .   .

Blessings. We rarely saw grasshoppers in the city when I was a kid. (Avoid local color if it's merely special pleading or a way of making privileged claims. Okay if it's a door to hell or heaven.) Summer was muggy, smelly, but also enchanted, for there would be lightning bugs and, once in a while, a grasshopper. The grasshopper's juice was holy fluid. When we caught one, we held its head to our palm and chanted: *Spitabacker spitabacker spit upon me.* If he blessed you, you had to release him at once or pollute the source. The other blessing medium was manure. Fruitmongers and milkmen still used horsedrawn wagons. In summer there seemed always to be warm glistening heaps fresh in the street, or dry flaky mashes blown by hot gusts. Sooner or later every one of us kids stepped accidentally in one or the other. But a person struck with great unearned luck, we said, must have been rolling in horseshit.

. . .

Briggflatts. The poet "lies with one to long for another, / sick, self-maimed, self-hating, / obstinate, mating / beauty with squalor to beget lines still-born." A statement of the restless, pilgrim nature of imagination, always preferring the desire for *something else* over the actual. The poem itself keeps moving away from its own occasion, its apparent center, the remorse over a love that died fifty years before. "She has been with me fifty years." It shoots out and backwards, to stargazing, legendary adventure, navigation, ancient British history, to the crafts of stone-carving, poetry, and music-making, to memories of waking with the woman, of the poet's first sexual experience, of many kinds of wayfaring. And yet while putting down experiences past and present in the sequential orders of language, *Briggflatts* has an all-at-onceness unmatched by any other long poem. It has a sure sense of the lay of the language, as we speak of the lay of the land, a topography of the imagination's movements, its sudden pilgrimages to events and feelings at different stages of history and different points in the poet's life of feeling. The language converts all the centrifugal pilgrim elements in the poem—all that migratory desire—into a compacted presence, a cumulative instance. The occasional density of the language enacts and testifies to this. "Then is diffused in now." Like a geological record, the changes and movements of the past are present, are "at once," in the densely veined instant. All the activities of cultural and erotic patterning—farmwork, poetizing, exploration, artisanry, conquest—depend on a simultaneous stillness and flightiness, the pilgrim's stubbornness and homelessness, encyclopedic feeling cocooned inside the moment.

. . .

Motion picture images are invasive of consciousness in ways that paint-
ings, photographs, and lines of poetry are not. These are subversive and
insinuating; they imitate reality by transfiguring it. Motion picture
images don't imitate appearances, they replicate them, with an excruci-
ating intensity and saturatedness. (How we learn to tolerate those inten-
sities in our private and social lives is another matter.) They are a
superfluity, reiterating or repronouncing the world visually with such
concentrated energy and retinal suddenness that they cut into con-
sciousness as poems and pictures do not. Movie images can be more
repulsive, smothering, executive, or totalitarian in the way they deter-
mine the feeling tones of physical reality. They leave us feeling violated
or rescued or elated, but their effects do not have the moral conse-
quence that poetry has. Poetry critically influences the way we deliber-
ate on and differentiate among the particulars of the world. Movies
offer globalizing feeling, not the severe hyperattentiveness to nuance
and degree we get from lines of verse or from good painting. And yet
certain moments in movies, while giving up nothing of that invasive
power, have in them a kind of poetry. I'm thinking of compositions or
sequences that fill consciousness with a knowledge of mortality—
comic, violent, obscene, melodramatic, whatever the tone—and make
of such knowledge a gaiety. I mean the gaiety or joy of consciousness
that poetry can give. The quiet swordsman shot during the battle
against the brigands in *The Seven Samurai* falls as warriors since antiquity
are said to "fall," with a fated weightedness and gravity, like Homer's
princes who fall from their chariots and their armor clatters upon them
and darkness closes over their eyes. The samurai falls and the muddy
rainwater churns around him. At the end of *Children of Paradise* Baptiste
plunges helplessly through the crowd of Carnival revelers to reach and
call back Garance, who disappears in that sea. He is tossed and held
back by the tide of celebrants all dressed like his theatrical self, Pierrot.
His own stage image becomes an indiscriminate mass that prevents him
from reclaiming his lover. Marcello, in the last scene of *The Conformist*,

Out of Notebooks

188

sits in the street crib of a Roman male prostitute, having just learned that the man he thought he accidentally killed when he was a boy (which crime he thought to expiate by becoming a fascist collaborator and assassin) is still alive. He turns and looks over his shoulder. Behind him a fire burns. It's a Platonic turn, the mythic turn of the prisoners in the cave, away from the shadows cast by the firelight on the wall of the cave, to look beyond the fire to the reality it illuminates. It's a moment of political and moral recognition when agonized private conscience is suddenly jarred into relation with history. Then there is the comic moment in *Rear Window* when Grace Kelly, surprised by Raymond Burr as she searches his apartment for evidence of his wife's murder, wiggles her finger behind her back so that James Stewart (who loves Kelly but is reluctant to marry), viewing the scene from his window across the courtyard, can see the wedding band, the evidence of the lost wife. In that instant, Burr notices her surreptitious gesture, follows the line of sight, and sees the investigator-voyeur across the way. The triangulated moment of moral implication and comic mock marriage, binding all three characters in a compact of guilty knowledge. Ring, promise, gold, and the woe (and possible murder) that is in marriage.

◦   ◦   ◦

In a certain Australian tribe, boys about to be initiated are taken from their mothers by masked men who carry them outside the village, make them lie on the ground, then cover them entirely with sticks and branches. They are "buried" in order to create an artificial night, estranged from the familiar natural night with stars and moon. They are interred in that absolute darkness, surrounded by terrifying creatures, until the arrival of the god is signaled by the sound of bull-roarers. These states of being are repeated throughout the initiation period. Removal, burial, darkness and death, terror and the arrival of the god. The forms of poetry in a secular time are like that. In and of nature, they

yet are not natural, but cultural. That artificial surround, the hermeti-
cism of form, makes you all the more alert to the presence of gods and
their terrifying assistants. Unlike the initiate, the poet is not just the suf-
ferer and receptor, but also the respondent, giving shape to the formless
divine darkness. In the sounds of the poem coming into being, you hear
and pursue the sound of bull-roarers; the rough music of the poem in its
beginnings is the noise of the approaching deity.

.   .   .

I had nosebleeds when I was young, sometimes three or four a week. An
elbow tap in a street game could bring one on, but the real trouble was
that the bleeding wouldn't stop. The dominant taste of my childhood
was the beety aluminum flavor of blood trickling down my throat.
Often it happened without provocation. It felt like a visit. Once, past
midnight, the taste really was a taste, my pillow was wet with blood
running down my lips and chin. My parents packed it with cotton, I sat
with my head tilted back, adult voices rasped above me. I began to
choke on the blood, which by now was dripping through the saturated
cotton, so I was taken to the hospital. Spilling blood, I believed, was a
holy action. From catechism and the liturgy (or from my obsessive,
needy distortion of them), I believed that blood was the means to
redemption. The body was the medium for deliverance. (Hopkins' testi-
mony: "Thou hast bound bones and veins in me, fastened me flesh.")
Suffering in the nerves, however, was degrading and shameful; the fool
weeps for himself in a corner. But for blood to be loosened in me like
that was also a chaos, my worst fear. Blood was mined with a motion.
Somehow in my young consciousness that blood redemption and disor-
der became weirdly tied together. The New Testament seemed to
depict the lives of the disciples as patterned sequences, purposeful and
lucid, but I fretted over what must have been the real violence and
uncertainty of their circumstances. Later in my life Caravaggio would

seem an exemplary artist because he paints holiness as an uncontrolled fire that burns inside disheveled animals of appetite and blood. Sometimes reality appears in my dreams as a dense white three-dimensional composition, or object in space, composed of pieces which come unstuck, loosened into puzzle-piece fragments that fall away and float into incoherence. It terrifies me, because I know somehow in the dream that the reality I'm viewing is its own site, is my own consciousness, the planetarium of the skull. When it comes undone, it is the whole world, or all I know of the world, bleeding away.

· · ·

The power of second sight possessed by Johnny in the movie *The Dead Zone* is allegorical of the poet's work. His power is conferred, or rather he is delivered unto it, when a car accident puts him into a five-year coma. When he emerges from that chrysalis, he finds that touching a person releases images of peril from that person's past, future, or present. When the hospital nurse checks his pulse, he sees flames in her daughter's bedroom and warns her in time to save the child. Johnny's consciousness becomes host to histories and destinies. His dominant humor is melancholia. Petrarch was a despairing melancholic lifted at times by arbitrary enthusiasms: "I find myself within the borders of two very different peoples from whence I can see both past and future." Ortega sums up his temperament: "Petrarch lived an indecisive life, coming and going from one to the other—*ora guardo davanti, ora guardo addietro.*" The present becomes an impassioned index or mediator or freezer compartment of past and future. Looking ahead, looking backwards, one *sees*.

· · ·

St. Paul, Romans 8:22: "The whole creation groaneth and travaileth in pain together." It's the pain of contingency, and yet we in developed nations take for granted comforts unthinkable one hundred years ago. We can live in relative ease without servants. Schools and churches are warm in winter, cool in summer. We have most of our teeth. We're not reminded indoors and out that we live in a world of shit and urine and garbage. Most people, at all levels of society, wear whole clothing and do not smell bad. Constantly present to us are images of glassy perfection, on TV and in movies, where action and consequence are perfectly timed and human beings practice behavior meant to be *watched*. What then groans and travails and we along with it? The perfections of civilization do not (yet) eliminate death and change. Postponements, concealments, mock transfigurations, and legends of death experienced outside the living body, these we know. We can dull or numb pain, as many indigenous peoples have known how to do for centuries, but we cannot eliminate it. The body is a world of hurts, a library or memory bank of pain. The passion of our technological imagination, however, seems more and more to be one that would abstract us from our world of pain and natural fact. Control and more control. It's human consciousness, anyway, that formulates that community and solidarity of suffering that Paul describes. The machinery of refinement may make our lives less constantly challenged by contingency, and so all the more reason to reckon that we are always one beat away from Paul's words.

◦ · ◦

I go walking in the hills early one morning with my friend R., a poet and editor. We see a few mule deer grazing in a clearing, a fat tarantula crossing the road, white spiders and their larvae on some devilish thistle, and a bobcat. Bobcats are shy and prefer to hunt in heavy brush, but this one was in the open, crossing a large meadow drilled all over by ground squirrels that had left hundreds of piles of dirt everywhere. The bobcat paused over a burrow, held still for a few minutes, and in a sudden blur held a flapping squirrel in its mouth. It looked straight at us then turned and walked back into the woods. Talking about it later, R. said how the event begged for a response, an answering poem. That if he brooded long enough it might yield something to him in words. We argued about that, because I'm skeptical, too skeptical for my own good, of charged opportune occasions. Poetry answers to the world's occasions, and attention to that reciprocal relation is the important work of self-preparation or readiness. But at the same time I feel ill-prepared and reluctant when an occasion seems too opportune, as if reality were presenting me with homework. The force of revelation for me is a gradual thing, not a sudden strike or cracking open of a chrysalis. Revelation comes when I'm able and prepared to watch and testify to the moral relations of the world. The relations matter more than melodramatic event. Revelation is serial recognition. I realized a bit later that for all our differences R. and I were really caught up in the nature of the offering—the morning light, the fragrance of bay laurel, the little powdery detonations in the field, the coming and going of the bobcat—and the *duty* we both felt to recognize it. The world's circumstance and chance had offered this to us, so what could we offer in reply? Words that remake and restore the occasion? Words that preserve the image of the time? Or that invoke the God in the scene?

◦　◦　◦

Attention is not an act of will, it's an instinct to hold on to what's given.

I teach, I explain, I talk talk talk. A student asks a question near the end of term. So I talk and talk, trying to clarify the issue, whatever it is. I feel, as I usually do (awake or dreaming), that I'm failing to express, failing to explain. So I ask finally: "Do you understand what I'm trying to say?" "No," the student answers. "But that's okay. I never understand anything you say."

Out of Notebooks

East and west. Fairfield Porter's art criticism has a flinty, patrician mat-
ter-of-factness that suggests a mind bemused by its own certainty. "An
artist who seeks subject matter is like a person who cannot get up in the
morning until he understands the purpose of life. Subject matter is
given: in his field and in his capacity as artist, the artist seeks grace."
This passage, like much of his writing, has the arrogance of recognition,
of whatever is candid and clean-cut, spoken as if by a cocky well-bred
college senior. And yet Porter did not simply allow for feeling in art, he
gave it central importance. He had a Yankee diffidence about the
vocabulary of spiritual concerns, however. His mention of grace, accu-
rate and sincere, is plain as wintry New England things are plain. He
always seems a little embarrassed, intellectually and emotionally, by
California things, which in his writings are mentioned as if they were
strange imports—dreamy, delinquent, irresponsible—from another
country whose authenticity was always questionable. He was really an
Atlantic islander, for whom things western—Bay Area figurative art of
the 1960s, for instance—were more or less Hawaiian.

• • •

—You're always quoting this or that dead personage. So and so said
blah blah but I think doo dee doo. It's all reaction, nothing original.
Pathetical dialecticality! Be more sociable, quote the great ones of our
time. Everybody knows who they be.
—Are you talking to *me*?

• • •

I publish in a magazine an adaptation of Leopardi's "A Silvia," his elegy
on the death of a young girl. A few weeks later (in November 1988) I
receive an anonymous letter from someone in Boston:

Dear Mr. Di Piero,

Instead of writing maudlin poetry (i.e., "Leopardi's 'A Silvia'")—not inspired but lamenting—why not simply live out your vision? Why not simply live as if all the ideals in this poem were alive and true? Why not crush everything that does not comply with this sublime vision? We need our dreams to become real; we need our dreamy visions here and now; we need to annihilate the endless parody of magazine, television, and their dreary imagery of whorish, vain women offering up their bodies for material use at the drop of a hat. We need our dreams to be absolutely realized—not lamented.

Best regards,

———

How to answer this? Silvia is not vain and whorish as TV images of women often are, but she *is* "of material use" to Leopardi. That may be a cruelty, though not a deliberate one, that poets sometimes perform, but it's cruelty that is finally made over into something else, it has to be. Leopardi's poem *is* a poem of grief, but it's also self-absorbed. The poem grieves over nature's broken promises, to both Silvia and young Giacomo. Was the letter writer suggesting in a sarcastic way that I should act on my "dreams," that is, on the nineteenth-century rhetoric I was adapting, and be a woman hater or woman killer? I've read this letter many times because it really disturbs and challenges the assumptions I have about writing. That there is a difference between ordinary daily truth speech and the way in which poetry seeks to express truth (or show what it's like to seek a way of telling the truth), that authenticity of experience and truth of feeling are refigured in poetry, not to distort or turn inspiration into something self-serving or self-absolving, but to intensify, to pitch more clearly and deliberately and complexly a truth of feeling. I sometimes think everything I've done since receiving that (slightly incoherent) letter has been done as a means of drafting an impossible reply to it. I threw away that version anyway. Later on I wrote a prose poem called "22nd Street" which draws on material from Leopardi's poem but is about a girl I once knew. It doesn't matter if it's not to the liking of my anonymous letter writer. It does matter that I have testified, in the way of poetry, to the trouble in a certain life.

                         ⋄ ⋄ ⋄

Ruskin, writing in *Val D'Arno*: "Writers and painters of the Classic school set down nothing but what is known to be true, and set it down in the perfectest manner possible in their way, and are thenceforward authorities from whom there is no appeal. Romantic writers and painters, on the contrary, express themselves under the impulse of passions which may indeed lead them to the discovery of new truths, or to the more delightful arrangements or presentment of things already known: but their work, however brilliant or lovely, remains imperfect, and without authority." Most art in our century has been post-Romantic, then, driven by the impulse of whatever is uncertain, unstable, brilliantly or garishly imperfect or raw from the world. But a lot of recent poetry and painting asserts certainty and knowingness. Now at the end of the century, we may be more susceptible that ever to fake sophrosyne, more needy of final authorities and formal certainties. We still look through pieces of the broken lens of authority. As if to give us a critical precept for moral thinking and feeling in our time, Nietzsche insisted that there were no facts, only perspectives on facts. Poets now more than ever, maybe in response to this, offer personal experience or uniqueness of sensibility as the only authority from which there is no appeal. It's a mongrel version of classical need crossed with Romantic profligacy and solipsism. Ruskin contrived his categories at the end of the century. At the end of ours, we cannot trust the contrivance of these or any categories. We want no more types or classes of things, only instances. (This sounds like Pater, another turn of the century rhapsodist.) And yet a poet needs patterns of instances, and will, if necessary, make or contrive such patterns.

Arnold Hauser takes this up in *Mannerism*. The classical, he says, synthesizes and concentrates. It wants only what is essential to a recognition of a reality, dismissing from its picture of reality "everything inessential, accidental, and marginal, everything disturbing, bewildering, or irrelevant. All the marks of the adventitious, the improvised, and the provisional have been eliminated from its formal structure." To this he opposes not Romanticism but Mannerist art, the art of Tintoretto, Pontormo, Parmigianino, and El Greco, and the poetry of Valéry, Shakespeare, Petrarch, the Metaphysicals, Tasso, and Baudelaire, which does not aspire to the unitary authoritative completeness of classical art, but values instead multiplicity, infinite variety, and exquisiteness: "A mannerist work is not so much a picture of reality as a collection of contributions to such a picture. The more original, the stranger, the more sophisticated, the more puzzling, the more demanding these are to the discriminating mind, the greater is their value." Universal validity does not matter. Let the fragmentary, the privileged, and the provisional be representative and general. Hauser exquisitely characterizes a lot of the poetry and painting of our time, or at least the assumptions behind it. I also feel, though, that the nostalgia for the unitary, for authority, for the centered coherence and truth of facts, can be heard in the peculiar exhortations of our poetry, the insistence on the commonality of experience in the sound of the "we," the sacerdotal tone of observation that would confer on random bits of the material world an aura of whole authority. The postmodern offers if nothing else an escape from this useless and ineffectual nostalgia. Escape, however, to what?

∘ ∘ ∘

Out of Notebooks

The most rigorous "formalists" of our time are not the so-called New Formalists but the Language poets, who handle words the way formalist painters handle paint, not for its referential authority or representational dynamics but for the action or dynamics of the material itself. Also like formalist painters, Language poets treat art as problematic: writing poetry is not primarily expressive, it is a kind of diagnostic display of those "problems" that are given to us with the use of language in our time. Wittgenstein is more a covering genius of their practice than Bergson. What is the pictorial identity of a statement in words? "You cannot say what you cannot say." These poets are at least confronting the issues raised by philosophers of language, issues which sooner or later have consequences for the words of poetry. But Language poetry is not very satisfying, and not post-Romantic enough perhaps. For all the unintelligibility of the poems—if we expect poems to give intelligible reports of reality—they seem perfect and complete in their problematic nature.

° ° °

As children we smirked at the rich Italian obscenities adults spoke. We longed for the just occasion to exclaim "*Ma vaffanculo!*" though we pronounced it in the southern manner so that it sounded as it's now phoneticized in popular culture: *Va fangoo*. But just as common was "*Ma vaffanabb'*" [*Va a fare a Napoli*], which I understood to mean, roughly, "Fuck you and fuck Naples, too!" Ah, nostalgia for the old country. The good life, warm bread, good wine, roasted peppers, and fresh tomatoes. Ah. In *Padre Padrone*, as a bunch of young illiterate Sardinian shepherds are being transported away to be inducted into military service, we see their haunted landscape, the rugged plains and hills and oak trees. The soundtrack sings of the lovely old oaks of Sardinia, while the young men, watching the trees recede into the distance, stand in the back of the truck, unzip, and piss in the direction of those noble oaks, the plains, and all the culture of impoverished misery they are happily leaving behind. Whenever I shyly asked my mother the meaning of *Vaffanabb'*, she told me that it meant "Go to work."

 .   .   .

The great collection of French painting from the Barnes Foundation is broken up and packaged for a touring exhibition, the first time paintings have left the Foundation established by Alfred Barnes several decades ago at his residence in Merion, Pennsylvania. Its first venue was the National Gallery in Washington, D.C. Only the flashiest items were selected. (The Foundation's holdings include Italian, Dutch, Spanish, and American painting, as well as decorative arts, ironwares, and tapestries, but museum directors know that Americans love modern French painting more than any other.) I was in the National Gallery on opening day. The large Tintoretto-esque dancers Matisse painted for the lunettes in the main salon now hung in the denatured culture-space of the museum, disoriented and abstracted. The next day the *Washington Post* carried stories about the opening. The tone of spectators seeing the paintings for the first time was mostly peevish, resentful that Barnes had "selfishly" kept these masterpieces "all to himself." But for many years anyone willing to reserve a time and make the short trip (easy by car or train or bus) from Philadelphia could spend leisurely hours with the collection. And of course students at the Foundation *used* the paintings as study aids. But that proprietary veil of seclusion was enough to insult many people's democratic sense. (Also because Barnes stipulated that the paintings could never be reproduced in color, so that the privileged "aura" of the paintings seemed even more remote.) Many who made the trip to Merion, expecting I suppose museum conditions, were horrified by the ambiance, the stuffy rooms, the "bad" lighting (one chandelier in the center of the large rooms, the rest natural light, to approximate,

Barnes felt, lighting conditions in which the artists themselves often worked). Whenever I've visited I've seen the works literally in a different light, depending on the season, time of day, and weather. The paintings always looked fresh and responsive, their subtleties dimmed or illuminated according to conditions. The outraged tone of the impatient spectators at the National Gallery suggests that Americans feel they have the *right* to see art treasures amassed by millionaire tycoons (who themselves have every right to do whatever's necessary to earn those millions). Someone like Barnes, who denied public general access to the aura of those paintings, was suspiciously un-American at worst, and an ungenerous creep at best. That Mr. Barnes was an ungenerous creep may very well be true. (He was evidently a very unpleasant man.) But it's grotesque to hear these sentiments expressed by Americans who would kill (or even file a law suit) to protect their rights of private ownership and the exclusivity that comes with that. But once a certain strain of beauty like Impressionist or Postimpressionist art becomes conventionalized in the public taste, it becomes tacitly the cultural share of the majority. French paintings acquired by a private person become, like TV programming, an American national treasure.

        o   o   o

In *Knowledge of the Higher Worlds* Rudolf Steiner says that one who becomes an initiate into higher knowledge does it utterly by "quiet attention and active reflection, and not by willful personal judgment." For an artist, this kind of suspension is difficult, maybe impossible, when the form-making instinct is one with meditative activity, with that "quiet attention," because the form-making instinct is also driven and steered by the will. It's an old question. Is it possible to pursue the knowledge of higher orders, as Yeats and Oscar Milosz and H.D. did, and also make poems and images which take so much of their essential vitality from dross, from the contingency, impurity, and anarchy of what is given? I usually fail to achieve in the words of poetry an intenser spiritual realization, because I'm too hungry for mere things.

Oscar Milosz is interesting because he believed that verse, if practiced by an initiate like himself, was the work of reporting the vision already acquired, the higher knowledge already attained. There is no Way in his poetry, as there was for Dante, no walking up and down and around. In the *Trilogy*, H.D. takes herself through the stages of recognition of a new life, a renewal of consciousness in the way we re-vision myth. She was writing her way out of the devastations, material and spiritual, of World War II. Her poem moves in its stately way through the stages of her own neediness, awareness, puzzlement, and self-doubt. It was Milosz, though, who said something that perfectly describes Dante's poem, its formal action, when he spoke of thought as "an awareness and love of movement." That is what matters most, the movement, the action of the blood in forms. But I have no affinity for the Milosz who says: "I have seen. He who has seen stops thinking and feeling. He can only describe what he has seen."

.   .   .

Philip Larkin's poetry is exactly what his admirers want it (and him) to be. Melancholy but never impolitely or menacingly so. Worldly but cynical about his own worldliness. Capable of appreciating the appeal of aspiration, especially the desire for transcendence, but thank heavens sensible enough to know how rotten and feckless such aspiration is. Endlessly self-critical, impregnably knowing, reluctantly (but endlessly) self-absolving. He cannily understood what would most attract readers. He let nobody down, purging moral surprise from his work (while insisting on his own fatigued moral intelligence) as if it were the most useless task of all. He deserves his most eloquent admirers.

.   .   .

Out of Notebooks

Love's redemption is not answerable to reason, theory, or will. We collapse into it. The way down points the way up. When Raskolnikov, doing hard labor in Siberia in punishment for his crime, literally collapses into unconditional love, Dostoyevsky describes it thus: "How it happened he himself did not know, but suddenly it was as if something lifted him and flung him down at [Sonya's] feet" (in the superb Pevear/Volokhonsky translation). Moments later, when they realize that the seven years of Raskolnikov's imprisonment would be at once unbearable suffering and infinite happiness, Dostoyevsky comments: "But he was risen and he knew it." Risen like Lazarus, whose story so obsesses R. earlier in the novel. Raskolnikov, wrapped wormlike in the cerements of nihilism, of Napoleonic conceits, willfulness, and awful nervous anguish, is finally freed *without reason* to arise. Falling at Sonya's feet, he is exalted. Both actions become one movement of the Soul and its love. Shestov says (in *Job's Balances*) that Dostoyevsky renounces certainty and makes uncertainty his most sought-after goal: "That is why Dostoyevsky simply puts out his tongue at evidence, why he lauds caprice, unconditional, unforeseen, always irrational, and makes mock of all the human virtues." That is how we come to know God, through uncertainty, unreason, and a festive mockery of evidence and proofs.

. . .

My feeling for inadequacy. Giacometti is the hero of our time, practicing the passion and joy of form-finding while also convinced that everything fails. The work is bound to fall short of what the imagination wants it to become. I've lived so long with these convictions that they begin to feel like a romance or a consoling manner. In *All Things Are Possible*, Shestov writes: "Creative activity is a continual progression from failure to failure, and the condition of the creator is usually one of uncertainty, mistrust, and shattered nerves. The more serious and original the task which a man sets himself, the more tormenting the self-misgiving." What prevents this from becoming a pathology or depressive state is the joyfulness of misgiving, the vigorous (though sometimes manic and debilitating) movement of the soul at play among its form-seeking doubts. If the activity is kept in motion, if the soul doesn't lose its delight in play, the act of misgiving won't become a manner or regnant mood.

. . .

One purpose of meter is not to help me find my way through a poem but to help me lose my way. Not to write poems that illustrate formal principles or theories but poems that are themselves expressive formal events. Make a poem an image, not an illustration.

. . .

Nietzsche and Wittgenstein. They practiced philosophy in a way that makes them models for poets: they systematically and joyfully philosophized against themselves.

. . .

In Book VIII of *The Metamorphoses*, Daedalus warns Icarus to fly a middle course:

> Don't go too low, or water will weigh the wings down;
> Don't go too high, or the sun's fire will burn them.
> Keep to the middle way.

The technologue's sound advice to the artist, which the artist then has to reject. Typical fatherly advice, too. No wonder poets envy engineers. So much power amassed in the middle, wadded and cunningly balanced there. In "The Flower" Williams complains to his lover that it makes him

sick to see how quickly a new bridge can be built while he can't find
time to get a book written:

> They have the power,
>
> that's all, she replied. That's what you all
> want. If you can't get it, acknowledge
>
> at least what it is. And they're not
> going to give it to you.

◦ ◦ ◦

I met a famous critical theorist who said that when she taught at the
University of Iowa many of the poets from the Writing Program attend-
ed her courses and were among her most clever and interested students.
I said that I thought critical theory turned poems into illustrations of
ideas, a language equivalent of conceptual art. Poetry deriving from the-
ory sounds too much like knowing, self-serving puzzlement. Relativism
or perspectivism can itself become authoritarian. The usefulness of the-
ory probably lies in its tenacious skepticisms, its refusal to let old ways
of thinking pass unquestioned, challenging poetry, painting, and ideolo-
gy whenever they begin to seem (in Iris Murdoch's phrase) "too naively
and soothingly referential."

(Poetry may question the nature of reality, but I think above all it wants
to express the feeling of putting such questions and of living with that
uncertainty.)

◦ ◦ ◦

On being a nobody. What if books of poetry were published according
to the "Barnes Principle"? In the Barnes Foundation, the pictures have no

wall labels identifying artist, title, date, style, circumstance, etc. A single artist's works are not grouped together but spread among others. One wall displays a Tintoretto, a Renoir, a Cézanne, and one or two works by lesser artists of different periods. I imagine books of poetry made available to the public without illustrious dustjackets, blurbs, bios, medals of merit embossed on the cover, hysterical reviews, etc. That way, everybody becomes a nobody, except for the singularity and expressiveness of the offering in the words.

What if books and pamphlets were, as someone has proposed, displayed at supermarket checkout counters? Yes, but let them be displayed anonymously in plain wrappers. Browse and shop, shop and buy. Let the poet who suggested that, and the poet suggesting this, be the first to have their works so displayed.

◇ ◇ ◇

Re-reading "The Prisoner of Chillon," one of the poems that really possessed me when I was a boy. It struck me then, as it probably strikes most children, with the blunt force of noble suffering. (It also had a fullness of feeling and an ornamental flair that nothing in my culture had prepared me for.) It's not very good poetry; it suppresses and conventionalizes what is most anarchic and aristocratically scornful in Byron's intelligence. It sounds, in fact, a bit too much like Edwin Muir's poetry, though Muir's gift was his ability to convey complicated decencies. For Byron, conventional decencies, however courageous and complex, are glazed with obscenity or diabolical ridicule. Muir never laughed in his poems, and Byron is mostly laughter, even in *Manfred* and *Cain*.

◇ ◇ ◇

For me, it's a useless piety to live in search of subject matter and become impatient with reality if it does not provide provide provide. Reality does not possess or contain meaning. It is meaning. The poet who tries to cipher the emblems of meaning that reality encodes will, I think, sooner or later feel oxygen deprived, or "blocked." And yet what an exasperating task it is, to want a torrential inclusiveness of the glory and density of existence *and also* the selective, deliberative, sorting and patterning adjudications of the moral intelligence, the pliable intelligence by which life in all its processual messiness comes alive in the mind and along the nerves. To want both the "all" and the "only this," the alarming entirety and the judicious bit, the running stream and the bright knobby twig riding the current.

. . .

Louise Bogan's prose in *Journey Around My Room* has the lyric signature of her poetry. Her mind had such an economy of passion, a compactness, a tartness even, that after reading too much of her I begin to feel the force of the denials in that fastidiousness and precision. Every word in the journals seems *put* there, placed with pursed deliberateness. Nothing casual, whimsical, or accidental. At least, nothing is allowed to seem that way. J. V. Cunningham, who admired Bogan's work, himself left little or nothing to chance. Instead of "All choice is error," he might have written, "All chance is error." I think it must be possible to be rough-cut in one's work, even disheveled or untidy, and yet sacrifice nothing to imprecision or inaccuracy. I admire very much Bogan's and Cunningham's dense austerities of feeling, of religious and erotic feeling especially, and the sensuous arguments their poetry conducts. I like W. S. Graham's poetry for the same reasons. But such an art wants juice, or juiciness.

. . .

So much pressure coming from the universities, the mass media, and from art forms like photography and painting, to be theoretical, conceptual, *diagnostic*. In other arts, an idea of an artwork is sufficient to make something, anything, so. How many poems do we see now that are more or less ideas or conceptualizations of poems? Better to be expressive, front and center, blatant, even rude. Like Ruskin, rudest of the rude, who says in *Praeterita*: "Accuracy of diction means accuracy of sensation, and precision of accent, precision of feeling."

. . .

One of my favorite movie scenes occurs in Hitchcock's *Sabotage*, his adaptation of Conrad's *The Secret Agent*. A Scotland Yard inspector, investigating a cell of conspirators in wartime London, walks down the side aisle of the Bijou Cinema, owned by Mr. Verloc, who lives with his family on the premises. We track the agent as he moves, catching his slant view of the screen, its twitchy shadows and lights, the audience rapt and laughing. He then sneaks behind the screen to eavesdrop on the saboteurs meeting in Verloc's lodgings. When he inserts himself behind the illusion, the image we saw moments ago projected on the front of the screen we now see looming on the verso, gross and tissuey and hyperbolic. Its power to control group emotion seems all the more grotesque and scary when we see the massive wafered image close-up, depthless and wraithlike. We hear what the inspector hears. On one side, the vivid social life of image fiction—the projector's throaty roll, the audience's rustling amazement; on the other, voices which have power to bring death to innocents. (Later, the young brother of Verloc's wife, unknowingly transporting a terrorist bomb to Picadilly Circus along with film reels of *Bartholomew the Strangler*, is killed when the bomb goes off in a crowded, slow moving bus.) The cozy preserve of the moviehouse rumbles happily just a few steps from the kind of terrorist intent that can turn a Bijou into a shambles.

Out of Notebooks

From when I was a kid, spending weekends at double features, I've loved moviehouses for their shared secrecy, anonymous company, and unmenacing spookiness. Even now, in my overlit suburban multiplex, I feel the same queasy anticipation before the big screen that awaits its images. When I've moved from place to place, I always pay an early visit to the local moviehouse, to eavesdrop on the conversation up there on screen. Testifying to big manipulative moving images in a big dark room feels like the first stage of local citizenship. My ritual is, I suppose, an example of the way the drama of moviegoing is inseparable from our sense of "the movies." We wrap narratives of our presence or involvement or the stage of our lives around the narrative of the picture itself. We *contain* moviegoing in a candid, social, often urgent, always intimate but shareable way. In the early 1970s, at the old Telegraph Repertory in Berkeley, a showing of Sam Peckinpah's *The Wild Bunch* (the most complete version of which I had seen at the Embassy in San Francisco, an exquisitely decrepit and now defunct Market Street movie palace that doubled as a relatively safe flophouse for winos, druggies, and transients like me, and where we all got to participate in the "Big Wheel!" contest spin that interrupted evening shows) was followed by riotous cries of "Fascist bullshit!" countered by equally vehement shouts of "This is real American art!" A few nights later, while I waited to squeeze into a small auditorium to see a clandestine print of the then sequestered *Titicut Follies*, a young man behind me talked thrillingly about finally seeing that excruciating and legendary documentary about conditions in a state-operated insane asylum, but along with that he speed-babbled some anecdote about Callas singing *Tosca*, bits of which he explosively sang (in beautiful Italian) even while nattering about the forbidden document we were all about to see. Social unrest was different then from what we see around us now, more anarchic, voluble, and historically informed, and it was not defined or contained by social and economic class. Around that same time, multiplex cinemas were coming into vogue. Ironically, they began when art houses carved themselves into multiple viewing chambers to accommodate more independent and foreign pictures, or to show mainstream movies that would offset the expense of showing less conventional work. Culture atrophies if it doesn't change, and change brings the pangs or pains of the unfamiliar displacing what's known and rosy. I try not to get cranky at my local multiplex when the feature is projected on a curved screen designed to accommodate the satellite-pod viewing rooms spoked around a huge central lobby that functions as a combined mess hall and video arcade. This particular multiplex, constructed on a strip of land between a freeway and marshy bayshore, was built to serve communities, my own working-class suburb among them, on the mid-Peninsula south of San Francisco. Mushroomed there at land's end, in an enormous parking lot along a row of car dealerships and unfinished furniture outlets, my multiplex lies nearly two miles from our small downtown and is called an "Entertainment Center," though it's not the center of anything. While its ambiance and offerings have adapted to (and helped mold) suburban habits, it has kept at least one traditional social function. It's a place where you know you can always find people. And so last summer when angry teenagers from one of our neighborhoods wanted to find the boy they felt had "dissed" them, they drove by the multiplex at 1 P.M. of a sunny day and fired into the available teenage crowd. One adaptation of the suburban multiplex is to have made itself, by virtue of its physical isolation, a good shooting gallery. Inside the center are video games imaging mock firepower of very imaginative kinds, and beyond these are the cinemas themselves. On their screens, behind which lie no spaces for investigators or saboteurs, firearms of the most ingenious designs are being gleefully fired at all shapes and sizes of human beings, and at mock humans, too, at holographic and androidal and virtually real human beings, and at molten humanoids that can revivify themselves so that they may be shot again. What kind of nostalgia will someday make this memory's favorite home-place?

◦ ◦ ◦

Out of Notebooks

Coleridge's letter to the Wordsworth household, where he confesses to "sinkings and misgivings, alienations from the Spirit of Hope, obscure withdrawings out of life . . . a wish to retire into stoniness and to stir not, or to be diffused upon the winds & have no individual existence." That's just half the cycle, and in me it's not stoniness but muddiness, rubbery, dense, adhesive, impossible to rise from. The other part of the cycle is the wild pushy uncontrollable *activity*, speed babble, a helium delight in the smallest changes of daily life, the sick excitement of staying in motion and keeping the things of the world in motion around me.

. . .

When is poetry illustration?
—When in its descriptions it values originality too much.
—When peculiarity or singularity of anecdote is presented as visionary feeling.
—When its forms are didactic.
—When it puffs up particulars into universals.
—When it allows no reader to admire it as much as it admires itself.

. . .

Cindy Sherman's new pictures are of dummies, anatomical models from medical supply stores, splayed on their backs, twisted, or hitched up on all fours with their rear ends pedantically displayed. The sexual organs, nightmarishly oversized detachable vulvas and penises, are at once brutally explicit and demurely instructive. In some pictures, Sherman's own head, bewigged and made-up like a "painted woman," seems screwed to the top of a dummy body, or balanced there like a lightbulb in a shooting gallery. Like most of her work, it's Statement Art. The image idea must be as compelling as the image itself. The idea is that of the body reified, a mock-up controlled by gross sexuality. She makes the body look like a prosthesis of consciousness. Sherman's art watches us as we watch it. It's a kind of moral surveillance, or vigilante art, fish-eyed, taunting, daring us to make a wrong move or think a bad or inappropriate thought. Sherman's photographs don't pounce on my nerves the way work by Graciela Iturbide or Richard Misrach does. Its passion is mediated, and muffled, by its ideas. It's head-ridden, hermetic, and driven by conceit. I'm partial to images possessed of some kind of eventfulness, even if it's the eventfulness of an abstract pattern found. I don't like art, whether pictures or poetry, that scolds. I always feel a little ashamed of candor about the body when I look at Sherman's pictures. Maybe they are meant to intensify self-consciousness in that way, but they are also chastising and abstract. She scolds, in a mostly haunted or gleeful way, about not thinking enough about how we think of the body. But so much thinking about the body is enough already! Postmodernist feeling at its most severe and watchful insists that we narrow the range of acceptable thoughts about certain subjects. In the end it's a question to all of us: How much self-consciousness and diagnosis can any artist tolerate before self-consciousness inflects primary feeling out of existence? There is some correlative to all of this in our poetry, which offers so many solemn affectless pronouncements of what is self-evident.

◦ ◦ ◦

What we think of as crises or "critical junctures" in the history of poetry are merely instances among many others that poets lived through. We take what is given and work within its astounding limits. We experience not crises but plain familiar difficulty and practical inadequacy. There's no theatricality in that.

◦ ◦ ◦

Much of Paul Celan's poetry, as far as I can tell from the Hamburger translations, seems made of strategies and agonies of avoidance and refusal. The language has the kind of clenched willfulness used by someone prepared to take issue with anything said and who refuses to draw conclusions. The very act of making statements, Celan's work implies, must be resisted because it was made to serve Nazism's genocidal policies. The German language Celan inherited was a picture of atrocity. Yet he wanted to make a poetry responsive to atrocity, conscientious of history, alive with uncertainty and grief, and at the same time to dismantle the authoritarian patterns of the language. In translation his poems read like mechanically contrived complexes of evocation and observation. I feel I'm reading a coded text, though it's not the same code in which the original is enclosed. Every gnarled or broken or compacted phrase sounds like agonized testimony to inadequacy.

◦ ◦ ◦

Killing and control. Megadeath movies like *Robocop* and *The Terminator,* but also westerns and cop pictures and movies that dramatize the exhilaration of killing blent with social chastisement (like recent pictures about black and Latino gang cultures), essentially celebrate the power over creation that guns allow, one of our themes in America. The Judge in Cormac McCarthy's *Blood Meridian* gives voice to it. Educated, polyglot, knowledgeable of the names and natural histories of things, the seven-foot-tall, chalky white, hairless cowboy is the best-informed killer of a gang of scalp hunters in the 1840s. The Judge's morality tolerates only what exists by his sanction: "Whatever exists, whatever in creation exists without my knowledge exists without my consent. In order for the earth to be mine nothing must be permitted to occur upon it save by my dispensation." The decree of a God with a gun. It is the dispensation of murderousness. For all the "tender moments" in movies like those I mentioned, they are finally illustrations of the Judge's mind. Control through killing. In Homer, the word for work, *ergon*, is used to describe what men do in battle. The work of killing. The Judge's dispensation is the power that our audiences cheer and applaud.

◦ ◦ ◦

The things of the world, their chancy stirrings, all in motion, as the Soul is motion in the world. At certain moments there's suddenly a fused presence of times and things, stopped, as if on view before the Soul, staged there, while the Soul continues to move, too, before and around the vision. In a coffeeshop in North Beach, trying to concentrate on a book, the taste of the coffee distracts me, and the perspective of my view from the window, down the sidewalk, and toward the unseen Bay takes me out of myself. Like a laminate, the scene becomes one where I'm at a bar in my other favorite city, Bologna, twenty years ago. No two cities more unlike: hilly, fogswept, sunny, and open-faced San Francisco; recondite, medieval, porticoed, noble Bologna. The likes and unlikes all at once come together as one sensation. I have just read in my book: "Against whom do we struggle if not against our own double? Against that *other* in us who would have us believe that the world is without meaning?" The words are Bonnefoy's, the book a gift from E., who inscribed it to me, "who has something in common with this French poet." (But what exactly?) The Soul turns and stirs not to keep the *other* away but to engage it in conversation, in the motion of words and statements, for the recognition and its consequences keep me alive. Behind or above Bonnefoy's words are the waitresses' voices, Italian voices saying something about Santa Maria, just as church bells begin to strike. Is there a Chiesa di Santa Maria nearby? The bells toll in three-strike clusters, tentative almost, but finally with a satisfying, resolute balance and completion. What is this joy, so irrational and plain it makes me weep, to be here with these words of book and voice and with the taste of the cities and the bells? Time feels like a substance,

Out of Notebooks

something liquid coming into crystal, and at the same time it is a shadow, quickened, porous, unresistant, made of wind and light. The whole of it is what is merely given.

• • •

The mystery of details. The satisfaction of painted particulars. We enter a familiar museum or gallery and go at once (or pretend to drift) to a favorite picture, because in the picture is a detail we love, as we love lines or phrases in poems we can hardly remember the entire drift of. In the Frick I go to the Vermeer in the hallway, the one with the cavalier wearing a black hat. I go for the hat, mountainous, a landscape of fashion covering who knows what crucial details of the genre setting. Black of black, it determines the space in the painting and, strangely, makes for the intensest gaiety. When I visit Philadelphia, when I'm agitated by all the reminders of why I had to leave South Philadelphia so many years ago, I go to images that call me back to myself. Vitale da Bologna's little busybody *Crucifixion*. And Cézanne's *Large Bathers*, where the life of the flesh is made to seem sensuously complete in a landscape magisterially unfinished and incomplete. And the small Tintoretto self-portrait made when he was in his early twenties. It has the intensity of gaze that later would make his paintings of sacred events so disturbing; but the really great thing in the portrait is his *ear*, painted with a freedom and casual enthusiasm that I love. An artist's concentration is such that certain details will suddenly bear, unexpectedly, a full sense of existence. A hat, an ear, a phrase.

• • •

No wonder I'm so fond of San Francisco and Bologna, curved topographies (for all their differences) sloping or arcing or radiating from their epicenters. Growing up in Philadelphia, my geographical imagination had no curves. When I looked at the lush gibbous forms of Africa and South America, the little fleshy pendant of Florida, the floating debris of South Sea Islands, in my mind's eye they somehow turned into the Philadelphia street plan, grids, equidistant streets, rule-edged north by south and east by west, rowhouses, the rubbery staves of power lines over trackless trolleys, the gleaming iron trolleycar rails . . . . On our weekly visit to my aunts' houses in North Philadelphia, we drove on Sunday afternoon the seven miles straight up Broad Street, with only the semicircular curlicue around City Hall to interrupt that Puritan pursuit. When I left the city, I wanted only curves and spirals and bellies and hills. A flexing line extending infinitely in space.

o o o

I'll never get used to it, living in a suburb on the brittle crust of the West Coast, migrating once or twice a year to my South Philadelphia neighborhood and its tumultuous seasons. Here, sunshine, earthquake weather, cheaply constructed and ludicrously expensive houses, dense racial and ethnic mix, Spanish spoken everywhere. There, redbrick rowhouses fastidiously kept and tackily decorated (Gozzano's *"le buone cose di pessimo gusto"*), second generation Italian-Americans who speak no Italian or only bits of dialect. My soul more and more feels dropped into a cyberspace in which are blent those different structures, weathers, languages, the deep brown beaches of Atlantic City with the momentous closed faces of the casinos standing watch, the crumbling cliffs of the western shore with its harbor seals, elephant seals, and passing gray whales. One March, in Philadelphia, a great thunderstorm comes up. Purple sky, gleaming buds on dark trees. Lightning filaments split the sky in the chutes between skyscrapers, then the rain falls hard and heavy. But it's also something that, pouring down on me, shuts me out.

o o o

Out of Notebooks

In the 1920s Christopher Caudwell described the delusion of fin-de-siècle poets who saw themselves as rebels against capitalism and all its works, and who were easily absorbed "within the sphere of bourgeois categories" because the attitudes espoused in their poetry—extreme individualism and non-social character, exaltation of private fantasy and metaphor—took on commodity value of their own. Capitalist society conferred value on it precisely because it announced itself as singular, nonconformist, and revolutionary. Poets who pursued fame in the political-social context they claimed to denounce, and who made use of the same dynamic of publicity and exploitation they hated, produced an art that participated in the same capitalist relations it raged against. Caudwell called this sort of poet "the complete mirror revolutionary." Our own context is quite different. Poets, many of us, have the protection and institutional insulation of universities, but there is still that dynamic by which the eloquent and vituperative denunciation of privilege becomes a singular and ultimately privileging activity. Different world, same cynicism.

◦ ◦ ◦

For its enduring force and strength, the sacred doesn't require of us affirmation so much as the pursuit of what we humanly are, full of conflict and uncertainty. Poetry is possessed of some quality of the sacred when the patterns of its words embody the vitality of contradiction and strife. I recognize or sense the presence of the sacred most intensely when I'm most in conflict with myself.

◦ ◦ ◦

Labor Day, 1993. I go walking early evening in the park down the street. Two Little League diamonds, soccer field, softball fields, kiddie area. My neighborhood each year draws more immigrant peoples, from

Mexico, Salvador, Fiji Island, and India. As I walked in the almost dark I was drawn by the sound of voices singing sweetly but not harmoniously. A dozen or so Islanders, more or less mournful and more or less drunk, were singing songs of their country. Soon they were serenading me and the young family that had stopped to listen. A sad song, it seemed, but sung with some melancholy joy of remembrance. When I go to teach at the university I go to the Land of Abstraction. Theories about marginalized peoples, privileged texts and discourses, hegemonies and heterodoxies. I read an article by a critical theorist, a Latina, who compares her life as a marginalized person in the university to the station of domestic servants, yardworkers, farmworkers, and day laborers. In gnarled and nearly unintelligible professional language she writes of her moral and political identification with lettuce pickers and dishwashers. She is a full professor at a prestigious private university and makes, I suppose, a decent wage. Professional opportunism and the ordinary callowness that go along with life in the professoriat don't concern me. But what is the work of criticism? Not to practice an elite language and enthrone oneself in the executive manor of privileged unintelligibility. Not to claim to speak for the oppressed while using a language of the oppressor. It is somehow to listen to the woozy singing in the park and answer to it with equivalent plain intensity. The work of criticism ought to be to absorb and carry on—while observing and analyzing—that songfulness.

◦   ◦   ◦

Old Italian proverb:

> *L'uccello canta nella gabbia*
> *Non di gioia ma di rabbia!*

> The songbird in its cage
> Sings not for joy, but rage!

Out of Notebooks

INDEX

Index

McCarthy, Cormac, 212–13
McGrath, Thomas, 42, 45–53
Malatesta, Sigismondo, 31, 33
Mao Tse-tung, 51
Marconi, Guglielmo, 27, 28, 29
Maris, Willem, 106
Maritain, Jacques, 37
Marx, Harpo, 84
Marx, Karl, 51
Masaccio, 101–5, 110, 111, 170
Masolino, 101–3
Matisse, Henri, 118, 121, 123, 159–60,
   161, 164, 165, 199
Mauve, Anton, 106, 107
Mazzini, Giuseppe, 32
Merrill, James, 15
Metevsky (Sir Basil Zaharoff), 27, 28,
   29
Michelangelo, 101
Millay, Edna St. Vincent, 16, 91
Miller, Perry, 56
Milosz, Oscar V. de L., 200–201
Milton, John, 186
Misrach, Richard, 211
Mondrian, Piet, 167
Montale, Eugenio, 33
Moses, Gunther, 137
Muir, Edwin, 59–69, 167, 205
Munch, Edvard, 168–69
Murdoch, Iris, 83, 204
Mussolini, Benito, 32, 33

Neruda, Pablo, 46
Ness, Eliot, 88
Nietzsche, Friedrich, 14, 61, 64, 67, 196,
   203
Nixon, Richard, 184
Nizan, Paul, 14
Nolde, Emil, 121

Oppen, George, 34, 36–44
Ortega y Gasset, José, 14, 82, 83, 191

Park, David, 160
Parker, Charlie, 153

Parmigianino, 110, 117, 197
Pasolini, Pier Paolo, 10–14
Pater, Walter, 197
Paul, Saint, 191–92
Pavese, Cesare, 33
Peckinpah, Sam, 208
Petrarch, 191, 197
Pevear, Richard, 202
Philip the Fair, 27
Picasso, Pablo, 112
Pinsky, Robert, 56
Pissarro, Camille, 164–65
Pius XI, 28, 29
Poe, Edgar Allan, 16, 91
Polke, Sigmar, 115, 118
Pontormo, 197
Pope, Alexander, 87
Porter, Fairfield, 118, 163–64, 194
Pound, Ezra, 10, 19, 22, 23, 25–35, 43, 45,
   47, 52, 53, 186

Raleigh, Sir Walter, 71
Ransom, John Crowe, 186
Renoir, Pierre-Auguste, 205
Resika, Paul, 118–25
Rich, Adrienne, 54
Ridley, M.W., 108
Roelofs, Willem, 106
Rothenberg, Susan, 112, 166–68
Rothko, Mark, 160, 170
Rothschild family, 34
Rousseau, Henri, 119
Rousseau, Jean-Jacques, 175
Rushdie, Salman, 74, 75, 77
Ruskin, John, 80, 86, 93, 196, 207
Ryder, Albert Pinkham, 122

Salle, David, 118
Sandburg, Carl, 91
Sartre, Jean-Paul, 14
Savinio, Alberto, 115
Savinio, Ruggero, 115–16

Schapiro, Meyer, 133
Schnabel, Julian, 113, 118

Index

Index